AF392252

"A very lively bunch of stories with variations in structure, style and language to satisfy readers in both reflective and upbeat moods."

Polly Pattullo, Papillote Press

"Baptiste's style is natural and entertaining. His stories are grounded in everyday life with moral messages that are unmistakable."

Yvette Francis, Teacher

"The West Indian short story is an eclectic mixture of vernacular rhythm, colour, tone and style - an art form that should be preserved. And there is no better exponent than Lyndon Baptiste. His pace is unrelenting, gripping the reader to every word, fusing levity with the gravity of life's experiences. *Obeah* thrills, eliciting hearty laughs tempered only by the provocative reality of a practice still etched in the cultural DNA of a people. His wrenching commentary on the stench of wasted youth to ill gotten gains and violence is overwhelmingly haunting in *Simon and The Babylon*."

Dr. Glenville Ashby, author of The Believers

Boy Days

Lyndon Baptiste

Potbake Productions
Trincity, Trinidad and Tobago

Books may be ordered by contacting:

Potbake Productions
#3, 3rd Street West,
Beaulieu Avenue,
Trincity,
Trinidad,
West Indies
www.potbake.com
(868)640-0512
(868)487-9115

First published by Potbake Productions
ISBN: 978-976-95236-4-7

BY POTBAKE PRODUCTIONS

90 Days of Violence
Forward Ever! Backward Never!
oOh My Testicles!
Bend Foot Bailey
Across The Caribbean

Thanks to Lance and Louise Baptiste, Regina Cozier and Kimberly Badloo who were instrumental in improving this book. *Kimi*: I wrote all of these stories hoping to make you laugh or smile at least once. And to Lasana, my brother, a treasure chest of humorous anecdotes; *Tabby* and *Simon's rant* are his stories. *Alley-loo-yer* and *Flowers for Father* were written by my dad. My nephew Brandon is nine. He wrote *Man on a mission*.

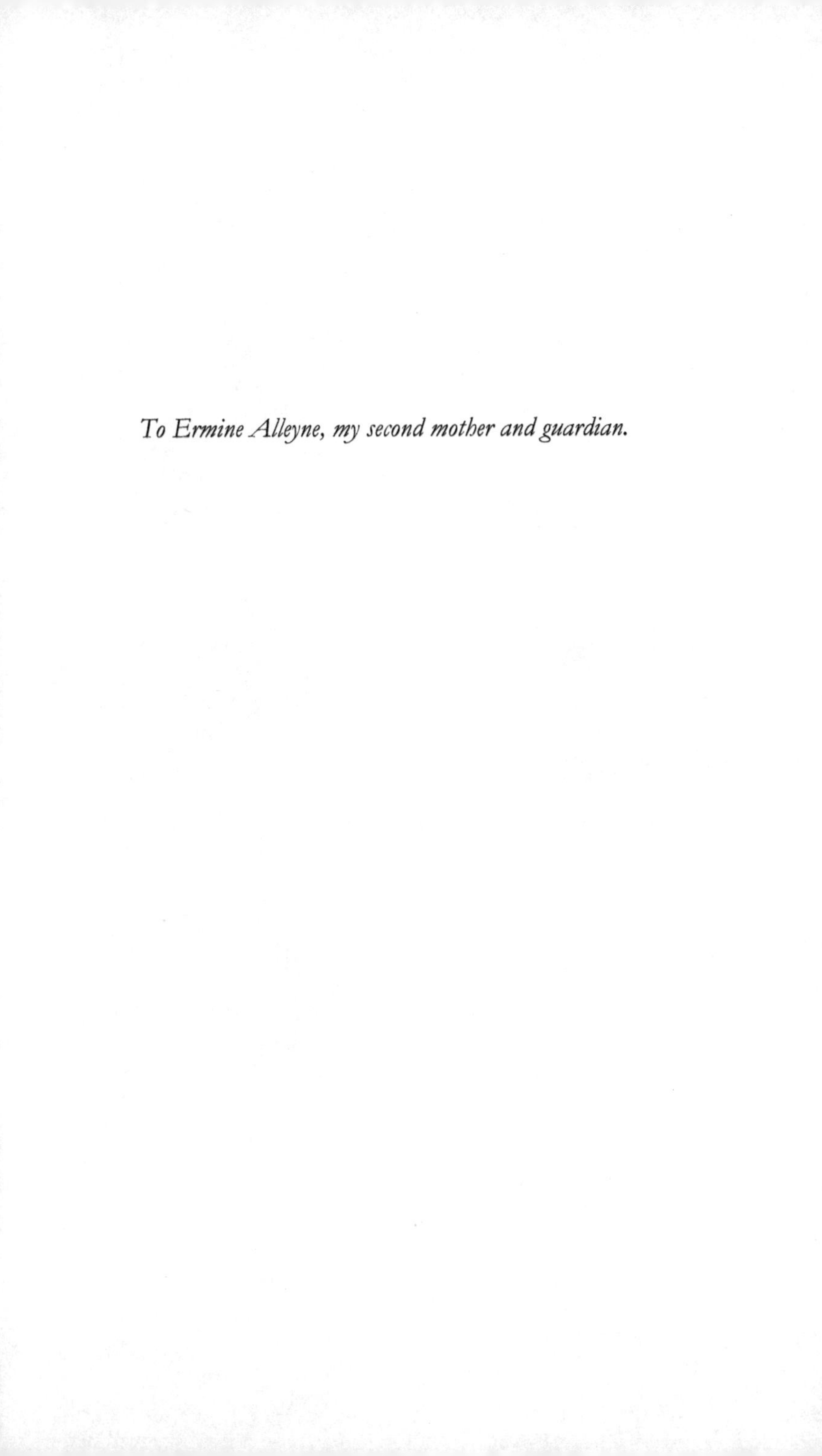

To Ermine Alleyne, my second mother and guardian.

Contents

Samo and his dulahins

No one in Dinsley Village knew his name. Even he had forgotten. He was East Indian, dark, with chubby cheeks, puffy eyes, bowl-cut hair and he walked like an oversized duck. When he was five someone nicknamed him Samo and pretty soon no one remembered why.

Samo's mother, a flamboyant prostitute, loved whiskey so naturally clients exploited her because alcohol was a cheaper commodity. Speculation had it that *Silver Fox*, a pony-tailed Chinese shopkeeper, was Samo's father. Samo grew up calling different men *pa* and he sought their notice but received none, except for slaps, taps, an occasional dollar, a drink of rum but despite the reward, men shooed him outside then did as they pleased with his mother. After her death Samo seemed clueless of her living even though some villagers heckled him nonstop. Still, Samo thought life quite pleasant with the exception of school. "Common sense better than book sense," he often told Nat, a classmate, friend and drinking buddy; every school term they fought for the last two positions in exams. Samo quit school before standard three.

Naturally Samo's life seemed miserable yet he won hearts effortlessly. He ran errands for villagers and they returned his kindnesses: women dished Samo leftovers and men invited him to river *limes* where he plucked and gutted chickens and ducks. When strangers hailed Samo he joined them and sang for drinks. Neighbours took him to Chutney shows featuring Bollywood singers, providing he toted the coolers.

Samo appreciated classical music; however he found true joy in Chutney which he sang like *the* professionals when pissing drunk. He gravitated towards the repetitive nature of these English songs flavoured with East Indian melodies. By age twenty-nine Samo sang Chutney better than most Trinidadians speak English. His lyrics knew no end. While singing he'd point and rub his stomach and depending on the rhythm he'd pitch his waist or spin as if with a dance partner.

Because of his antics Samo was a favourite at weddings. Cars came from as far as Penal and Cedros and whisked him away regardless of his attire; Samo always wore black dress pants, short sleeved shirts unbuttoned at the top and rubber slippers. Once rituals finished, guests lured him onstage. He'd lick his hand, slick back his hair and swagger towards the microphone. He feigned hesitation by stroking his goatee then erupted into song, swaying crowds with groovy tunes that slowed and saddened as dawn approached. Samo performed as long as *Puncheon Rum* flowed. Often times though he protested half-heartedly with a wagging head and sheepish smile but *they* always had the solution: "Bring drinks!" And Samo, weakened by the prospect, entertained like a trained parrot. He never earned a dollar for his skill.

Samo made his living as a packer at an El Dorado grocery, a house refurbished with narrow aisles and an upstairs warehouse. Drunk or sober he held fast to labouring as his mother had taught him: "W'rk hard Samo beca's' har-d thing is the best." He went to work rum-sick every day. It bolstered his ego when he deciphered heavier items and double-bagged them. Hefting bags with his forefinger he'd think, I have common sense. He accompanied customers into maxi taxis or waiting cars if they wished. He sang to those he knew. Seniors living in the district had a special privilege: while Samo wheeled their groceries home he enquired about their health and family. When Samo wasn't tipped he still smiled sheepishly and bade customers, "Good day, miss or sir, and thank you."

The most important thing to Samo was that he always had money to drink. He and Nat drank whatever and wherever; and when the regulars had left, they sat in the darkest corner, Samo, head between his arms, drumming the table, tapping his feet and slurring in Hindi; Nat, beating and stroking a fifty-cent piece against a rum bottle, meanwhile mimicking a cymbal or shouting, "Gi'e them fire!" This happened everyday and when Samo didn't have money he credited drinks.

It was April, midnight and drizzling. Outside *Dinsley Restaurant and Bar*, a black pudding/souse vendor wrestled a wooden table into his battered station wagon after a profitable night. Inside, Samo and Nat sat at a table littered with bottles, glasses and a bowl with water inside and around it. Among this litter lay wax paper heaped with black pudding, like moist sausages, speckled with onions, garlic and *bhandania* pepper sauce. A suspended television played opening credits for a Bollywood classic Samo knew by heart. Gazing at Nat, he mimicked the Indian actors onscreen but froze and stared on hearing *a voice* the epiphany of male charm and general's authority. His head flopped around then suddenly steadied.

"Amitabh Bachchan!" he shouted.

"Tha's movie star!" Nat whooped.

Samo went into a trance and danced around Nat and all the furniture. He sipped a drink as he sat. Head rocked back and slapping his chest: "Tha's my hero."

"But Samo," Nat reasoned, "critically speaking from a clear point of view he is a handsome man, *betis* love him!" He pounced from his seat and, shoving Samo, "You don't *even* have a woman in y'u' life!"

Unfazed, Samo said, "Still, he is my star boy."

Nat turned his chair around and sat, pressing his chest into the backrest. "He does dead in movies too."

"A star boy don't *have-to-must-to* win. I's about who he save, who he make feel loved." Samo sang in Hindi then translated: "I feel safe because I feel loved."

Like a man summoned too often, Nat shouted, "Yes!" His pitch lowered, but his exasperation remained, "Bu' wha' you know 'bout love, Samo?"

Stroking his goatee, Samo hiccupped. "I know love outside this rumshop."

Distorting his features, Nat inhaled sharply. "I wonder how it will be when *you* ge' marr'ed."

"The *liming* will have to stop," Samo smiled, "bu' not the drinking!"

"No, not we drinking," Nat exhaled.

Half an hour of heavy consumption elapsed before Samo barely raised his hand and shouted for another bottle. The barkeeper brought the rum but complained about an existing tab when Samo smiled thinly and confessed he'd pay later.

"Plus i's closing time," the barman said. "Samo, your eyes bloodshot. You had enough. I's about time you and Nat wrap up."

"When the f'lm done," Samo said matter-of-factly.

Nat burped. "*Plus* we need ice."

They continued carousing and although Nat fell asleep, Samo watched all of *Muqaddar Ka Sikandar* with his head propped on a shoulder. After he dozed off the barman snapped the lock on the burglar proof gate. At dawn when Samo woke from his dream he was no longer Amitabh Bachchan searching for love and friendship. Nat had left behind a little rum. Samo drank from the bottle and, rinsing his mouth, cleared the table. He swallowed then limped to El Dorado, his head arched forward dangerously like a fishing rod under pressure, his feet shuffling behind with that awkward, mechanical jog peculiar to hooked alcoholics. At the grocery, management had hired a new cashier, a black Guyanese woman with gold front teeth and an earring in her nose; Samo fell in love.

"I will marry tha' woman," Samo vowed to Savita, the cashier he worked with. Savita was dark with a sharp nose, sunken eyes and long, shiny hair. She ignored him, grabbing tin goods from the conveyor, scanning and skating them down the ramp to Samo; as fast as they came he bagged and secured the commodities in a trolley beside him. Cold items came next. After parcelling two dozen eggs and five packets of liver, Samo double-bagged a turkey and, satisfied, smiled. The customer, a grumpy, bearded man, paid via debit card. He refused Samo's assistance and left with the trolley. Savita faced Samo.

"You remember him?" she asked, nodding at the grumpy, bearded man as he slithered past shoppers. "One *smart man* eh. Remember three Saturdays ago he paid me with counterfeit money? The manager take it out o' my salary." When the man disappeared Savita shrugged, glanced at the Guyanese cashier three workstations away and uttered a half-strangled sound of disbelief. "Samo," she joked, "good luck with Prapti."

"Prapti," Samo smiled. "So tha's she name."

"Earlier she cuss up Mr. Manager."

"He mus' be look for it," Samo scoffed, "and tha' don't, what is the word boy, *define* she."

"Samo, I don't like to *run* my mouth and I don't want to fight with you."

"Yes, because I is a lover not a fighter; I is a *liver* not a gizzard."

"Next please," Savita smiled, motioning towards an old lady. Meanwhile Prapti mesmerised Samo; he packed bottles with tins, and Clorox with flour. Smirking, he tested those bags holding soap powder and chickens. Samo helped the old lady outside and into a taxi. Gesturing like a policeman and dodging cars that didn't stop, he ambled across the main road to a nearby rumshop and credited a drink.

Samo re-entered the grocery and looked around confused. All eyes were on his and Savita's workstation where the grumpy, bearded man had returned and was querying his bill in a boisterous manner. Stamping the floor and even pounding the cash register he spat colourful language. A security guard inched closer but said nothing. The Manager was scolding Savita.

"Savita, I have no choice," he said. "The amount must be deducted from your salary." Three workstations away Prapti was checking money and laughing mockingly.

"Bu' boss, I cashed everything," Savita said, her eyes like wet glass, and Samo shrugged enquiringly.

"Wha' happen?" the man scoffed. "I ge' billed for turkey, egg and liver! When I reach by m' car, turkey fly 'way! Egg hatch and gone! Liver dead and bury! I's a good thing I double check!"

Samo covered his mouth. "Bu' I remember bagging two dozen eggs and five packet o' liver. I even double-bag the turkey."

The man scoffed again. "You sounding like you drunk!"

Mr. Manager folded his arms and tilted his head. "Y'u drinking on the job Samo?"

Samo lifted one arm and stepped back. "Boss, le' we deal with the re'l problem. Savita and I have no reason to t'ief."

"*Then* Samo, where are the customer's goods? In the bar?"

Samo hiccupped. "Boss y'u hearing but y'u not *listening*. This discussion is thing for behind closed doors, not in front customers or employees. Savita will feel embarrassed."

"Wha'ever," the customer shrugged, "I jus' wa' my turkey, eggs and liver."

"Samo!" Mr. Manager barked but then he paused, closed his eyes, inhaled. "Samo, jus' go and get a turkey, two dozen eggs and five packets of liver."

Samo did as instructed and the over-pleased customer stormed away. After Samo agreed to cover all losses he continued working but just couldn't get over the incident. He'd stop working and begin recounting the episode: how Savita sat *there*, cashing; how he stood *here*, bagging; how he parcelled the eggs and liver; how he even double-bagged the turkey then tested and placed it in the trolley; and how the customer refused his help. Throughout the day Samo worked this way, stopping, scratching his head, pointing, until Savita's grief ebbed into a sort of sad amusement for she admired Samo's antics and virtue. Late afternoon when business slowed she said:

"You remind me of my father."

"He mus' be a handsome man."

Savita smiled and tucked her hair behind her ears. "He is a good man. Both o' all y'u similar. Ever since my mother die' he trying to replace her."

"I remember your mother," Samo said. "She was very special." He crouched and stared into Savita's eyes. "You are a nice woman too."

"Oh stop it Samo," Savita blushed, "we wo'king."

"Yes, le' we wo'k before we los' a next turkey."

Seven o'clock that evening Samo discarded his problems with a stiff drink. He slicked his hair with spit and returned to the grocery. The cashiers were at their workstations tallying total sales. Samo approached Prapti. She must have flashed a golden smile for his heart melted and his puffy eyes widened. When the thickness in his throat settled he slobbered through a mournful Hindi love song. Scowling, Prapti glanced around: Mr. Manager had exited his office and stood on top the staircase; Savita stared.

"Wha' the hell wr'ng with yo', b'y?" Prapti shrieked. "Yo' want me *bax* yo' in yo'r head?"

Samo bellowed, *"Dil dhakda hai, toh kuch lafda hai oh yeh,"* working his hands as if adjusting a light bulb. *"Ever since I saw your face you've filled my days."*

Unimpressed, Prapti demanded, "You wo-r-kin' he-r-e?" Batting her eyelids she didn't wait for an answer. "Wha-t is yo'r name?"

He straightened, cocked his chin, said, "I am Samo," hiccupped and extended a hand. "The pleasure is mine."

"Yo' lo'k like a nice fellar," Prapti said, ignoring his courtesy. "You're a T-r-ini?"

"Ye–"

"Le' we ge' marr'ed Samo."

Samo and Prapti didn't waste time. He spent the following day hunting his birth paper. Next morning when he staggered into the Warden's Office in Tunapuna she was waiting impatiently; while they hung their wedding banns she cursed and slapped behind his head. Three weeks later the villagers sponsored Samo and Prapti a spectacular wedding. As guests ate Indian food served on *sahari* leaves, Samo entertained nonstop, singing and dancing as if powered by a perpetual battery. By dawn next morning he had done everything but consummate his marriage.

Prapti, Samo's wife, possessed gold teeth, an earring in her nose and a black heart: she demanded gifts Samo couldn't afford; she refused to sleep with him, saying he looked like a "Buck Man"; she never cleaned; she never cooked not even for herself; she cursed Samo willy-nilly until people stopped taking them to Chutney shows; she never reciprocated Samo's kindness. Nevertheless he revered her like a queen.

Three months later Nat visited, wearing only a red nylon shorts and yellow rubber slippers. He found Samo in his backyard clipping panties to a wire draped between the house and latrine. Underfoot were broken clothespins.

"She have y'u washing she thongs and all?" Nat hissed. "Like tha' *bump and patch* re'lly drive y'u mad."

Samo, smelling boozed, embraced Nat then stooped, retrieved a clothespin and, tiptoeing, hung a yellow undergarment by its crotch.

"Samo, where Prapti?" Nat demanded. "Le' me fix she ass!"

Without bending his knees Samo picked up an empty basket. "She went Immigration."

He and Nat stumbled across dry, uncomfortable gravel to the shed outside Samo's house. There was a makeshift table beside the front door but no chairs. While Nat stood on one side waiting for the obvious, Samo disappeared inside, fetched *the* alcoholic's gadgets and set the table with sophistication befit for a banquet.

"You promise' we will never stop drinking, Samo," Nat grumbled. His arms were folded. Between them were two glasses, a bowl heaped with ice and two rum bottles, one frosty with water, one heated with rum.

"It ain't stop, Nat. I's the *liming* stop."

"Samo, critically speaking from a clear point of view you talking shit! We ain't beat liquor in months!" Nat snatched the rum bottle, pressed it against his stomach for leverage and twisted the cap so it crackled until the seal broke. Slowly, he topped the cap with alcohol then flicked its contents to the ground, he and Samo subconsciously muttering their reverence to *the* spirits. Nat licked his palm where alcohol had spilled then filled his glass halfway.

After Samo topped his glass he said, "Nat, I married now, you is a bachelor. I have responsibility."

"Bu' I hear she don't even care 'bout you."

Samo, wagging his hand, said, "No Nat tha's not true, she does treat me re'l good. You can't talk about my wife tha' way, you can't do that–"

"Look, Samo," Nat sighed, "le' we drink to ease we mind."

"Yeah… all this talk," Samo shrugged, "le' we take one." They bumped glasses and drank without twisting their faces. After a shallow drink of cold water Samo pointed his glass at a mound of weedy gravel in the front yard. "You and I use to pitch marble in this selfsame yard."

"Tha' feel like so long ago." Nat was staring at the floor.

"My mother dead and gone. Look at me, Nat." Samo smiled. "At least it have a 'oman in the house again."

"Who's the woman, Prapti or you?" Frowning, Nat grunted. "So you re'lly happy?"

Samo's right hand went to his heart. Eyes closed, head bobbing, he bellowed in Hindi. He smiled and opened his eyes. "She has freed me."

Nat helped himself to a straight. "What about me Samo?"

"I free' you Nat." Samo accepted the frosty rum bottle filled with water. "I see you open a chicken depot."

Nat scowled, "Y'u see the sign or depot?"

At that moment Prapti appeared, a mangy dog tailing her. She wore a mini skirt and nose ring like a fishhook. She zipped past without a sound except for, "Humph!" The dog stopped before the shed, growled dangerously at Nat, barked at Samo.

"Shush nah dog!" Samo pleaded but when Prapti screamed from inside that *he* should shush *his* ass, he shouted an apology.

"She's a real bitch, boy." Nat slammed down his glass and kicked mockingly at the mangy dog which scampered away, dipped its head and barked, dodging invisible stones Nat scooped up and flung until weary. "And you love *that*, Samo?"

"Nat, my only ambition is to make Prapti happy–and drink rum till I die."

"Nah boy Samo! Something re'lly wrong with you." Nat downed his drink and rubbed his lower back as if in pain. Wordlessly he turned and walked away. Cursing, he flung another invisible stone at the mangy dog and took a giant step over a deep, narrow drain that passed in front Samo's house. As he stumbled along, his red shorts and brown skin appearing and disappearing between the leaves of a hibiscus hedge in front Samo's yard, he gestured, shrugged and mumbled to himself. Finally he vanished.

Samo secured his drinking gadgets in the clothesbasket, exhaled and stepped inside an unpainted concrete unit he called home. The wooden window was shut and the room smelled like cigarettes and vomit. There was a grimy stove, small refrigerator and cardboard box with empty rum bottles at the foot of a spring bed with two mattresses. No bed sheet. Clothes piled up in the centre. Wounded pillows, naked and showing sponge. Prapti sat on the bed, legs crossed, smoking and reading a legal document. She ignored Samo until he approached the bed and began folding her clothes.

"Wha' *S nat* wa' doing he-r-e?" she demanded.

Bobbing his head like Amitabh Bachchan, Samo said, "Ah, Prapti, Nat is my friend."

"Bu' I tol' y'u I don't wan' 'nybody here. He's no damn good!" She tapped cigarette ashes onto the vinyl floor. "Imagin' y'u h're drinkin' rum and I in the blas'ed sun!"

"Ah, Prapti!" Samo tilted his head and bobbed it crazily like a broken doll; he closed his eyes and sang: "Save—"

"Don't y'u sing, you h'ar?" Prapti dropped her cigarette and Samo stubbed it out with his slipper. "Don't set y'ur face like tha'," she barked. "Y'u does lo'k like a black *Elvis*."

Samo burst into song but Prapti, standing suddenly, bawled: "I fed up o' y'u shit!" She slapped Samo and went outside. With one arm folded she fanned herself. "I fed up wa't on Immigration!" She lit a cigarette and wandered off with the mangy dog.

Three weeks later after earning her Trinidadian citizenship, Prapti abandoned Samo. Five days later when there was still no news of Prapti or the mangy dog, not even at work, Samo stumbled to Nat's house one street away. Nat had fenced his property. The front gate opened outwards and two hanging signs declared "Open" and "Halal Chicken". A concrete counter with white tiles as small as stamps separated Nat from customers. On top were plucked chickens wrapped tight in plastic and a paint bucket filled with clean water, a yellow rag lapping over its brim. Further back were buckets of hot water and barrels caked with feathers and blood. The depot smelled fresh despite an overpowering Clorox blanket. Nat, back turned, stood draining the blood of a headless chicken into a blue barrel. When the chicken ceased its hopeless flapping he ambled across his workspace going past a hanging scale and hose coiled on the ground, spouting water, blood plopping behind. He dipped the chicken in a bucket topped with steaming water.

Samo was very dramatic. "Nat," he wailed, "she leave me, oh gosh Nat she gone and lef' me!"

"Le' Indian pull they bow," Nat said. He had dropped the chicken. Removing his apron he went to the counter, leaned over and forcefully embraced Samo. "Come le' we go and take a drink."

Nat closed shop and when he and Samo presented themselves at *Dallas*, men lifted their brows. Samo called for a bottle on credit and the drinking began. After the drinking and singing, a bitter argument ensued and Samo and Nat would have fought if not for the barman. While Nat simmered, Samo mumbled and grumbled then fell asleep. Next morning he purposely woke before Nat, drained the rum bottle and stumbled to work.

At work everyone knew of Samo's predicament with Prapti but the other Guyanese women were unsympathetic. They concluded Samo was their ticket to Trinidad citizenship. They pursued Samo relentlessly. In five years Samo cycled through eight more cantankerous Guyanese women. Somehow his weddings were always lavish and his divorces discreet. Whenever these women secured their papers they left Samo and he went to Nat; the chicken depot closed and they drank every day until Samo married again. On the night of Samo's tenth marriage, Nat, misty-eyed and wearing no shirt, cornered him.

"Samo, critically speaking from a clear point of view, you have fowl brains or wha'? You know i's papers she want!"

"Nat, I don't care," Samo cried. "At least I doing something good for them."

"What them ever do good for you?" Nat scoffed. "You sleep with any o' them?"

Lips folded, Samo wagged his head. "An' I don't need to. When I think about their life my heart does melt like butter on a hot roti. Some o' them does have to lif' groceries to feed they family." He tilted dangerously toward Nat and shared this secret: "Mr. Manager does have sex with them though. Y-e-a-h… tha's he wo'k! Not mine!"

Nat palmed his forehead and slid his hand through thinning hair. "I *doh* understand your maths *nah* but know this Samo: I love y'u like a hog love mud."

Samo smiled and his head began bobbing. *"Kaise dil dil dedon yeh mera ab nahi! How can I give you my heart?* It's no more mine." He interlocked his fingers behind Nat's neck, tugged him closer and when their foreheads met, Samo whispered, "Come le' we go and meet my *dulahin*. She's a beautiful girl from Georgetown. She name… I *cyar* even remember wha' the jail it is." He kissed Nat on his forehead and supporting each other they went searching for the bride.

Samo found her dancing. She wore a red and white sari with gold trimmings, and no shoes. Mehndi and bangles decorated her hands and feet. Around her a crowd clapped and whistled. Samo slid behind his bride and discovered her hands and when she knew it was him her fingers tightened and they danced as if alone.

"Who are you?" Samo whispered, his mouth pressed against her neck.

She laughed as if tickled and keeping her hands in his turned to face him. "I am *Savita*," she whispered back. "I am *your* dulahin."

"Ah, Savita, it is you," Samo smiled.

"Yes Samo it is me Savita. Did you eat?"

Samo set his face as if food sickened him. "If I eat I *go cyar* drink again." When Savita smiled and stroked his cheek, he nudged his face against the back of her hand. "Will you like me to sing for you Savita?"

Savita stopped dancing but still held Samo. "No *dulaha.*"

Samo glanced around. People circled *now*, laughing and mimicking their gyrating. A man holding a microphone embraced and massaged Samo and encouraged him to sing but Samo consulted his wife:

"Do you want them to leave?"

"Yes Samo."

"Nat too?"

"*Everyone* must leave. Our noise is not for their ears." Samo smiled, sheepishly, and although it took time he cajoled happy people off his property using the microphone.

Samo and Savita consummated their marriage.

Next morning he woke three hours after dawn and made breakfast while she watched him. Before marrying she had disinfected and cleaned the house.

"It is strange," Savita said, "that we have worked together for fifteen years–"

"And never knew we loved each other?"

Savita turned to her side and propped herself up on an elbow. She sat up and wrapped her naked body in a white blanket. "Samo," she whispered, "I have loved you ever since."

Samo worked on the wooden table, slicing tomatoes into quarter moons. He stopped and smiled at Savita. "Why?"

She leaned forward, her black hair tumbling over her shoulders, the white blanket knotted above her breasts. "You really don't know, Samo?"

He picked up a whole tomato. "I *really* don't know."

She stood and embraced Samo from behind. Pressing her cheek against his back she squeezed him and sighed as a lover does. "Because despite everything you have a good heart. Do you know I love you, Samo? Tell me you know it."

"I know it."

She turned him and held his face. "Say it like you mean it, Samo."

"I *know it.*"

Savita smiled. "Now, what do you want for lunch? Shall I bake the turkey?" While speaking, she unlatched and pushed open the window until it snagged the outside wall.

Samo had glanced away when harsh white light filtered inside. "Mr. Manager really gave us a turkey?"

Savita laughed, adjusted the blanket above her breasts and knotted it firmer. "It is a sentimental gift, perhaps, his way of making peace. However, it is too large for our refrigerator."

"I will take it by Nat," Samo said. "Do we have work today?"

Savita shook her head.

Samo poured water into a blue basin filled with flour and sitting beside the cutting board with sliced tomatoes on top. "While I prepare this dough tell me about Savita. There is much I don't know."

Savita told Samo her parents were Guyanese but she was Trinidad-born. She spoke of her mother's loss to malaria. Her eyes saddened when she spoke of her father's futile quest for love, his luck with devilish women, his return to Guyana. "He is lost. Where? I do not know."

Samo appeared distracted. "Lost and loveless."

"Everyone is lost without love." Savita flicked on the gas tank and lit the back burner. "Is something wrong, Samo?"

Samo removed his hands from the dough and flicked ten fingers over the bowl. He was staring into the flour. "Savita, you wan' me to stop drinking?"

She moved closer and held his wrists. "Look at me, Samo. As much as you would like to although, yes, that would be nice."

"Savita, I go stop drinking," Samo said, "*for you.*"

Savita said nothing. Later that night after she cooked *baigan chokhaa* and *sada roti* and they had eaten, she and Samo nestled on one chair below the shed. Around them trees rustled. Overhead, an enhancing glow circled the moon. Savita surprised Samo with her lyrics. His tunes won her heart years ago, she sang, caressing his face and goatee. '*Kya kahana hai kya sunna hai: what is there to say, what is there to hear?*' Samo reminded Savita he'd never drink again; still, she said nothing.

Next morning after Samo shaved his goatee he double bagged the turkey crowding the small refrigerator and limped to Nat's house. When Samo shouted for him he appeared, wielding a cutlass as if prepared to use it.

"*Jeez-an-ages* Samo, *doh* tell me this one gone wit' you' beard!"

"No," Samo smiled, sadly, "I come to tell y'u tha' I stop drinking."

Nat studied Samo. "I now going an' say le' we go by the rumshop."

"Le' we go," Samo said. "I could go and not drink."

Samo abandoned the turkey and Nat closed shop. Samo credited two bottles by *Las Vegas Bar*. At midnight Nat and Samo took a third bottle to the latter's home. Inside, Savita was sitting on the bed folding clothes. When she heard their commotion she stuck her head past the front door: Samo held Nat in a headlock. They stumbled and, just as quickly, recovered. Propped against the table Samo sang, "Rum kill me mother; rum kill me father!" and Nat, still struggling to get free, joined in, "Rum kill Samo's w-h-o-l-e *family!*" When Nat spotted Savita, he sang, "Savita kill Samo."

"Ah, Savita," Samo slurred, "come take a drink with y'u' *dulaha.*"

Not showing any disappointment, Savita said: "Samo, you promised to stop drinking but—"

"*But* is a conjunction," Samo interjected and Nat scoffed, "You now learn tha'?"

Savita wrapped her hair into a bun, switched off the outside light and, pulling a chair behind her, joined Samo and Nat in the darkness. Samo said something unintelligible.

"How you going, Nat?" Savita asked.

Nat scoffed when Samo said, "I *never* promise *myself*, I promise *you.*"

"Don't do that, Samo," Savita said, "don't make promises you can't keep."

"I should go," Nat stuttered, pushing down on his chair's armrest.

Savita stopped him, "No Nat, you sit down. You is part o' this."

"Savita, y'u shaming me in front my friend," Samo mumbled and counting slowly on his fingers, "It is only *uno, dos, tres* bottles we drink."

When Savita hopped her chair closer Samo raised his feet and dropped them like planks on her lap. She embraced him and, stroking his hair, whispered: "I never asked you to stop drinking, Samo. I came into this marriage knowing *you.* I love you." She released him, smiled then fetched three glasses and a bowl with ice from inside.

"You wa' me sing?" Samo asked and not waiting shouted for backup. He rapped the table and Nat joined in, shrieking like many cymbals; and when their rhythm stopped momentarily, Savita's crescendo humming blossomed into balanced, beautiful Hindi; *Yeh Dosti* she sang.

Weeks later, under Savita's firm guidance, the three friends formed a musical group and played nationwide at weddings and competitions. Six months later *The Dinsley All Stars* secured $100,000 at the National Chutney Monarch with their nationwide hit: *Leave me, but leave my rum.*

Everyone whispered Samo had found his place but he truly matured two years later when Savita swelled with child. Next day after packing groceries, Samo walked around heralding the news and clearing his debts at village rumshops. After, he visited Nat to share his joy and request a favour. Samo celebrated with one drink and Nat agreed to help. Two months later Samo and Savita moved into Nat's home and a local builder demolished Samo's mother's house. Five months later, a modest concrete house stood on tall pillars. The builder installed a fence and gate then Samo and Savita moved into their new home. Three weeks later when Savita gave birth to a boy, Samo sat below a poui tree with pink blossoms and wrote *Save one: me; and save one: you.*

When Samo and family returned home, villagers waiting below the house greeted and assisted them upstairs. Savita sat in bed with her legs stretched out, a pillow below her feet, another at her back, cradling her son, cute, wrinkly, two weeks premature but healthy. Samo stood guard, distributing hand sanitiser and surgical masks to visitors. Towards sundown, Nat visited, a rum bottle peeking out his pants pocket.

"Yes Samo, at leas' you sure tha' chil' is yours," he joked. "Wha' is he name?"

Savita shrugged at her husband.

Samo sang crescendo, "Elvis Samaroo," then baritone, "jus' like he father," and Nat, tapping the rum bottle with a fifty-cent piece, urged, "Gi'e them fire," and Samo bellowed, "Elvis Samaroo jus' like he father." Nat shrugged, took a drink and shoved the bottle at Samo, saying, "Here, y'u need a *strong*," but Samo refused, singing, "Leave out the rum, I have a son," and Savita joined, "Leave out the rum, *we* have a son."

"Critically speaking from a clear point of view," Nat stuttered, "wha' *stupidness* all y'u re'lly singing?"

Smiling sheepishly, Samo went over to the bed, stroked Savita's cheek and kissed *Little* Elvis Samaroo.

Linda

Trini men like to believe they lucky with a particular race o' woman, a specific breed: the reds, whitey, Indian, darkie, Spanish thing from Columbia, or *dougla*. But this belief flawed because *he* always think he "lucky" with the *type* of woman he attracted to.

You should know I read that because I can't talk so high level. Is m' partner who explain me. My name is Inshan and I is the kind of fellar who really attracted to *dougla* girls, that sweet, tantalising mix between Creole and Indian that does kind o' force you to stop, and bite your lip, and gauge *this* woman, and say, "Yes, family, you re'lly looking good!" And you don't mind that she pass you straight, shading she eyes and admiring she toes, because y'u done know Trinidadian women don't know how to accept compliments, except, of course, if is from a man who have a lil colour, or he handsome, or looking like he have money in the bank. But back to these *dougla* girls. For me is like you getting the best of both worlds, the details of which I go leave out.

I not lucky with darkies at all, so one day, to my great surprise, I meet Linda, one chocolate empress, African to the bone, shiny black with teeth like dinner mints, although from behind, because she weave straight and glossy like plastic, I take she for what we in Trinidad does call a Madras, with a big bottom. I meet Linda when I went to deposit my first pay check, mind you my salary so small I getting paid with petty cash. The girl crop up in the line behind me. She looking good I will not lie, but I don't want she feel too nice so I *study* rubbing sweat in my hand and looking for she reflection. Anyway, that not working. Somebody touch my arm. When I turn 'roun' she watching me through two big *googly* eye. She voice lil heavy for a girl:

"You could hold this spot for me?"

I don't even have time to say yes, the girl skip over the bar and gone outside. Mind you, people start to line up and I only telling them how somebody right behind me. When Linda come back, she hand me a bottle of water and say thanks. Well I shock for the water. I doubting it have people so nice. I say:

"Darkie, you hitting on me or what?"

The girl swell up she face so big a blood clot appear in she eye. "Because I buy a bottle of water for you?" She vex, water running down the side o' she mouth.

She stun me, but I recover nicely, "You could o' just ask me to lunch!" I add a laugh and that smooth the tension. We stand up there talking and we even eat something together as I had two sandwich in my bag.

While we waiting, we arrange to go out Saturday. My mind working fast. I want to make sure everything in place. Phone number? Check! Name and surname? Check! Watch she one more time to make sure she nice? Check! Three o'clock we meeting in Tunapuna, in front FCB? Check! Ring she cell phone there-and-then to make sure I have the right digits? Check! I rubbing the money in my pocket because I want to buy a lil old car, but I duck out the line and tell she we on; cinema sounded good to her.

Saturday morning, your one and only Inshan, still surprised that a sweet Creole thing check for *him*, organise himself nice and gone down Tunapuna for two o'clock. Well, to my surprise, Linda waiting, decked out in a tight, blue jeans and a fruity strapless top that hugging she assets like an Australian teddy bear does hug up a tree. I saying to myself, boy Inshan, you is the man! I tell she how the bus run early for once and me and she start walking to the cinema, my salary secure in my back pocket with rubber band wrap 'roun' it in case anybody try to pick m' pocket. Every time we pass a clothes store Linda stopping and saying, in a funny kind o' way, like she want me feel bad:

"Hmm boy! Inshan? I like this dress. What you think?"

My responses:

"Too long!"

"Nah! Too short!"

"Too cheap looking."

"Too dark for your complexion."

She grab my hand and drag me inside a clothes store. She pick up a skirt looking like a towel. My eye nearly pop out when I see the price: one hundred dollars.

"Hmm boy! Inshan? I like this skirt. What you think?"

"Yeah man." I was studying how to change the topic. I pick up a five dollars panty; it squeaked. "What about this?"

"I don't want it, but my sister go like it. Buy two."

I happy to leave the store. Of all things to happen, a *snowcone* man stan'ing up just after Charran's Bookstore. I make a joke with him but he didn't laugh and he say something in Hindi I miss. Linda order a *snowcone* with condense milk, but she not making a move to pay. She walk off and I had was to dip in my pocket.

I hoping she ain't see nothing she want before we reach Monarch Cinema. Nex' thing the girl stop by Mama, a big fat roadside vendor, and buy a whole pack o' Dunhill. Linda light one and tell me to pay. Wha' I go do, boy? What you would o' do? You might be quick to say leave she *tail* right there, but if you remember how the story open you go understand why we keep walking. Just this time I worried. When we reach Monarch we there stand up, the line not so long, Linda in front, blowing smoke in my face and slurping she *snowcone*. When we reach the booth I buy one ticket.

Linda twist up she face. "Wha' is tha' one, dread?"

I say, "Linda, girl, you eat out your ticket."

Simon and The Babylon

My name is Simon and I born and grow up in a hole I does call The Gaza. I is a hustler, a pimp, a Gaza Youth. The Gaza have no skin colour; is all 'bout guns, money and level 'ho'es.

People outside The Gaza does say I don't have no ambition beyond gold guns and gold teeth, but tha's lie because *my mission* is to run the whole strip. Outside The Gaza it have no good wo'k for Trini youths like me. Who say otherwise damn lie! My mother does talk re'l crap too, saying how all that glitters is not gold, bu' she is a re'l player: she have three son for three different man. Me? I is the oldest. While other fellars was getting they education I was robbing them after school with a simple kitchen knife, plain talk and bad manners.

When I turn seventeen *I* pu' down a killing for a *big boy* name *Teeths*. I feel like a re'l man when he gi'e me the *nines* and say hold that! Is the bes' gift I ever get. *Teeths* promise me more jobs, more gold, but two days before a big wo'k, *Teeths* come and dead. He ge' seven shots to chest. Imagine, he own black brother kill him, tha' remind me o' a song I hear in a maxi, "Is the black man pulling the black man down." You *cyar* trust nobody this rounds.

With *Teeths* dead, things ge' kind o' rough. I have gold teeth, is true, but I *cyar* eat that. Plus I need a new sneakers. I see a *Jordans* in *town* I like for over a grand, bu' I only have six hundred in my name, so is just a lil hustling I have to do. One morning, while I sit down on the front steps cleaning my *nine*s, I watch maxis passing on the bus route. I study, bu' wait nah, them drivers does have re'l money on them.

Lunchtime tha' same day, I pu' on a denim kit and *Tims*. I slide my cap low over my eyes and tilt it to one side. My jeans riding below my boxers. I jump in a maxi coming from town; it only have one or two people in it. I sit down right behind the driver. A sweet *reds* on my right hand side. It have two people in the front. Jus' as we pass Arouca, I make my move. If I scared? Never scared! *I* take fellars' Ghost a'ready, wha's a lil robbery? I chook my *nine*s in he neck and I tell him to pass the money or he dead. If he was scared? *Humph*! I almos' laugh while I robbing him. Is nuff respect for me, dread. I rob three maxi tha' day. Later, I gone in town with a coil o' money in m' pocket, and buy two sneakers and level brands! If you see me blinging on the basketball court. Fellars scoping me out like they want to rob me, but they know I packing; nuff respect!

Two weeks later, I make papers big time: *The Bus Route Bandit*. I shake my head, yes dread. I take out the front page and stick it up in my room. Business ge' so good I start to rob the whole maxi. Me ain't like wo'king with nobody, bu' I pull in a youth man, *Tongues*. This is how we does operate: when we jump in the maxi, I does make sure tha' I sit down behind the driver. Tongues go sit down in the backseat. When the timing right, he go ring the bell, and from there is action!

Humph. Every robbery re'lly different, yes. A night a maxi man slam a brakes on we fo' spite, and I end up in the front seat. *Steups*, me and Tongues blaze he ass. A evening I had to bus' up a woman head because she child only bawling. One morning a driver shit *heself*, and the money in he back pocket. He ge' 'way.

Steups. As with everything else, them other fellars spoil things for we. They see it have re'l profit, nah. Hear this one, this one is the greatest: a day, two youth men board a big maxi in Curepe. When I tell y'u bandit mark on they face. One sit down next to me, the next one sit down three rows back. I flick up my collar, pull down my hat and I smiling and gauging them in the rearview mirror. They lil *antsy*. When we reach D'abadie the one next to me chook a Rambo knife in the driver neck and say:

"Gi'e me all y'u money."

I stick my gun in *he* neck. "Nah, is you who have it wrong." I blind him with my gold teeth. "Gi'e me all *your* flipping money."

In all the excitement, while Tongues fumbling to pull out he *nine*s, he shoot a small man wearing primary school clothes.

Later in the week, me and Tongues bounce up again. I was liming on my front steps with a page on m' lap and a pencil in my hand, writing a rant, smoking a joint, listening to Cutty Ranks spit lyrics on my cassette player. Inside, my mother quarreling 'bout a phone bill with some new jackass she hook up with. I gauging Tongues. He have a newspapers in he hand. He *cyar* even read. He scared. Is a look I *cyar* tolerate.

"*Dawg*, the 'mall man who we s'oot in a coma—"

I watch Tongues like he had to be joking. "Who *we* shoot, or who *you* shoot?"

Tongues scratch he face. "They s-ay he is a MP nephew."

I take the newspapers and pull out the page 'bout *The Bus Route Bandit*. "Wha's a MP?"

Tongues rock back and say, "To me I s-s-see tha' on a ketchup bottle."

"Tongues, you st-st-stupid or wha'? It must be mean Most Valuable Player."

"Bu' like is you who 'tupid? It have no V in MP, *dawg*."

I cuss Tongues and laugh. He sit down, we smoke two *ten piece* and when he cool out, we organise and rob a maxi. When we reach home, we hear two fellars from Barataria ge' shoot. In the night, Tongues call me on the house phone.

"Them two fellars who dead is the same two y'u take the Rambo knife from. I hear is police kill them, *Babylon* kill them! You feel is because of the small man who ge' s'oot?"

I sit down on my bed and light up a *blends*. I jus' talk to a red thing from Arima who say she belly big fo' me, so my head lil hot.

"Nah, boy, Tongues, tha' *cyar* be. A MP *cyar* have so much links with the police. I wonder if is them fellars from up the road? Nah… it *cyar* be. Tongues, *steups*, wha's your re'l scene, boy?"

"I running scared, *dawg*."

"Y'u 's a *chi chi man* or wha'?"

"Simon, I scared… later, *dog*."

Next morning, I hear while Tongues sleeping he ge' three shots to head. They out he *gyul* light too. Life have to go on… small thing. As I leaving for work, two police van pull up.

This Gaza Youth not going down easy. I run. I know The Gaza like the back o' my hand, but The Babylon jus' as fast. They wearing mask too. I bust through m' neighbour front door, cut through the side and shoot down a lil space between the house and a red bricks wall. I study to run across the highway and loss them in the dump, but two police van cut me off. My heart beating fast. I run back to m' house. Three police van in front.

I open fire on The Babylon. Is the second time in my life I blas' a gun: one shot, two shot, three shot, five! I prob'bly los' count 'roun' the same time bullets start hitting me in m' chest: *thud-thud-thud*. I look down and laugh. My gold chains red with blood — as if blood could be any other colour, y'u so damn stupid. My sneakers and all soak down. I *steups* and drop to one knee, still blas'ing shots. I manage to run across the highway, bu' I trip on my laces. Imagine that, a pimp like me lying in the *dutty*, stinking dump. I hear my mother bawling:

"Not my son, not my son!" She voice soun' far, jus' like it does be in the movies. "Oh God, Simon, talk to me, baby!"

I couldn't see she face, but remember me! *I* is a Gaza Youth! If anybody ever ask you how all them robbery start on the bus route, tell them 'bout Simon, the *dreadest* youth that ever pass through The Beet... I feeling tired; Gaza *fo'ever*, as one gone a nex' one born.

Obeah

One night I see a fellar I know in a party and when he make me out, he lift up his hands and shout, like I a mile away, "A-a! Wha' y'u saying, boy?" He throw me off a lil bit so I re'lly couldn't remember he name, and I shame to ask, so I introduce him to a *skirt* I was *liming* with, Anna; he shake she hand, like he know she long time, and is only when he do say Keith, I *steups* and laugh and we start to talk about schooldays. We there jibbing, the vibes nice, but when Anna excuse *sheself* and gone to the toilet, he grab my shoulder and whisper, "Boy, you know who she is? She not easy! She family does dabble in *thing.*"

"You mean drugs?" I ask, keeping my eyes on the toilet.

He laugh, "You go ahead," and some woman he was liming with hustle him away.

One month later, Ms. Anna and I get in one hell of a big argument. It went like this: the girl ge' me naked, fold up m' clothes and put them in a corner then tell me how she married and divorced.

I say, "You mean at the same time?"

She shake she head, yes.

I set my face like she ex-husband running me down with a cutlass. "Woman, you mad? I not in that!"

Anna more vex than me. She pelt my shoes and clothes behind me. She was breathing hard and only pointing at me, like a teacher who plan to cut a child tail good and proper. She disappear from the room and while I still slipping on my pants (I couldn't find my jockey shorts) she come back in the room with two Rottweiler that resemble Satan. I jump up on the bed, bawling, and when she le' them go, I high jump over they head, bust through the door and scramble through the house until I find the front door. Them dogs would o' tear me to pieces if I didn't jump from upstairs.

When I wake up next morning, I sick like a dog. A patch of my hair remain on the pillow, almost two handful. My toenails red, yellow and green, like a Rasta belt. I say, bu' wha' the jail is this, like I catch some kind o' gangrene, red eye and jaundice. Plus I have a rash that looking scornful. When I show my mother she tell me go doctor. Of all people to meet as I reach downstairs is Keith. He shocked to see me.

"What you doing here?" he ask.

"I should ask you that because I living here." I lil agitated. My skin scratching like mad.

He look at me like he couldn't tell I was in a hurry. "Wha' 'bout you and Anna?"

I laugh. "Boy, we done so long!"

He shocked, but looking glad. "You better watch yourself, eh, because she family does dabble with Obeah."

I gauge him, like we playing cards and I think he have a better hand. "This Obeah thing for real?"

"A-a! People foot does turn green and yellow and all kind o' thing."

I bawl out. "My two foot is them colours." I pull up my pants and show him.

He bawl too. "Yes aye! They catch y'u!" He ge' kind o' serious and ask if Anna had anything belonging to me.

I watch the sky and play the whole scene backwards in my head, from the time I jump over the banister to the time the two Rottweiler walk in the room, while I was pulling up my pants; I groan like a Bedford. "I think I fo'get my drawers by she, boy."

"You think? You better check and see if you have any rash." He pointed. "Down there!"

When I do check, I start to bawl again.

"I have to carry you by *Cornhusk*," he say. "Bring all the money you have," and it is the way how he say it, shaking he head, lips fold up, eyebrows raised, I know one time that *Cornhusk* was the only man who could help me. When I jump in his car, he end a call.

"I call *Cornhusk*." He sniff in my direction. "You mash dog *two-two* or wha'?"

Shaking my head, I check below my shoes. "No, horse!"

He smell under his arms and check below his rubber slippers. "Boy, you re'lly have a *light* on your head because y'u smelling like crap."

I scratch my head and a clump o' hair fall off. "Just hurry up and drive!"

Traffic was stiff to St. Joseph and Keith didn't want to put on the air-condition. We turn off the eastern main road and drive miles up inside Maracas until we come to a lonely side street with bush on the two sides. At the end of the road it had a rotten-down galvanise fence with grass pushing through the holes. On the gate it have a drawing of a chicken, and a sign: "*Mother Cornhusk*. By appointment only. Walk with yuh candle. Walk with yuh fowl cock. Love potions? Walk with two pig stones."

Keith pull up the handbrakes hard and say: "Right, we reach."

We jump out and he push back the gate, and I walk in first. I taking my time because I having second thoughts. The yard small and bushy, with a dirt track leading to a ramshackle house. The track lined with bamboo poles that holding up animal skulls. Other than that, is heaps and heaps o' beer bottles and telephone copper everywhere, and in the backyard it have a Rottweiler tied to a sapodilla tree, with branches extending over the house and front yard and sucking up all the daylight so the place looking like it late in the evening. On the lower branches, it have white sheets tie up like hammocks, as if is some kind o' trap for spirits. I inching my way along, past a rusty fridge, worried I get tetanus, when a voice stop me in m' tracks:

"Cease to move!"

I nearly *two-two* m' pants because the voice dark and it evil, and it could o' come from anywhere: the bush, the space below the house or behind me.

"You bring plenty evil here!" the voice continue, circling closer.

Mother Cornhusk appear in the gallery, a short, fat, black lady, wearing a white, white headtie and white, white dress. When I turn to run, she fly towards me and grab my face. She have a beard. I couldn't tell if she was *ah* Indian or *ah* Creole. She wearing hibiscus flowers around her neck and rings made of copper wire on every finger. Her clothes smelling strong o' Bugmat. *Mother Cornhusk* still holding m' face. She shake her fist, like she rolling a dice, then suddenly open her hand and shells scatter all over the ground in front me. She scream and jump back nearly taking my face with her. She make a cross with her hands, shout, "*Do so,*" and start to laugh.

"This one powerful," she tell Keith, "but I will deal with him." She wipe her nose and look at me. "Wha's your name, spirit?" When I tell her, she laugh. "So you have tricks too?"

She went down on all fours and draw a line between the both o' we.

"I sense a woman," she say, studying the shells and shaking up, like she getting shock, "a beautiful woman, who tell you she have no man, but she damn lie, because she damn marr'ed." She spring to her feet, bawling, "Your name is *Egungun!*"

Mother Cornhusk tell me to wait, disappear in the bush and return holding a length of rope. Before I could make a note, she start to offload some licks in m' tail. I start to bawl. I mus' be freak out after the second lash because I didn't remember hitting the ground. When I open my eye, *Mother Cornhusk* was standing up over me, eating a sapodilla. When I sit up, she laugh, throw away her sapodilla and pick up a piece o' cable.

"I exorcise you!" She screaming, dancing around, blazing my tail good and proper.

And I bawling: "Enough, enough! I exercised! I healed! Oh gosh! Help me!"

And Keith ain't moving a muscle.

"Get up!" *Mother Cornhusk* say. I jump; where I get the energy from, I don't know. "You need to get back your jockey shorts," she say, stroking her beard skilfully. Before I say anything, she raise her hand. "Do not worry. I know you cannot. Neither can you get one of her underwear." She put her hand on my shoulder. "You need a bottle of rum. That will be three hundred dollars."

I say, "That too expensive. I go buy it outside and come back."

"If you leave my domain," *Mother Cornhusk* warn, "we will have to start over from scratch."

I study the licks. "Bring the rum."

She lift up her skirt and take out a sealed bottle. "Take off your jockey shorts and shoes."

I open my eye big. I look at Keith. I look at *Mother Cornhusk*. "I could go inside?"

"No! My temple must not be defiled!"

I want the Obeah to work, so I take off my clothes, pulling down the front and back of m' jersey to hide my privates. *Mother Cornhusk* crack the seal, take a big drink then soak my shoes and jockey shorts with rum. She hand me the bottle, three-quarter empty.

"Put on your shoes and holey jockey shorts!" she say. "Good, take them off again. Now drink! Don't stop! Don't open your eyes!"

I feel a spirit coming over me. I into the process. I prancing around like I warming up, my eyes halfway rollup in m' head, and the liquor bu'ning m' throat. *Mother Cornhusk* start to chant like a Apache-Baptist. She disappear in the bush and return with a steel pipe, but when the rum finish, I scream and pelt the bottle clean over the house. Then, the spirit overtake me and I start to dance and while I dancing, *Mother Cornhusk* beating me like a dog, but I not feeling a thing, and with every lash the pipe bending more and more. Screaming, I lif' up the fridge like it weigh nothing and pelt it to the tip-top o' the sapodilla tree in the backyard – yes, y'u hear me right: *on top* the sapodilla tree.

Mother Cornhusk shout, "Run home, boy, run home and do not look back, the curse will only lift if you don't look back."

I run home, wearing a jersey on m' back and a jockey shorts on m' head. My mother was washing a pot. I lift it up and drink all the water. Then I went and sleep.

Next day I healed. Tha' Obeah thing does re'lly work, I telling y'u, I not asking y'u. Two months later, when I went a party with a *skirt* from church, I bounce up a fellar I went to school with who know Keith re'l good. He tell me how Keith and he *gyul*, Anna (the same one who le' go the two Rottweiler that resemble Satan) ge' lock up for beating a policeman with a pair o' pig stones. *Mother Cornhusk*, Anna's mother, was in hospital; a fridge had fall from a tree and break she two hand and foot. The fellar couldn't explain my Rasta-coloured toes or my hair loss, but when I brace him 'bout the rash, he tell me it was *cow-itch*, or something so, and the rum was the remedy. But he talking crap. Tha' Obeah thing does re'lly work.

Flowers for Father

Boy days. Happy days. Sad days. Crab, callaloo and dumpling days. Creole cocoa days. Bat and ball days. Gramophone days. Hugo Blanco's harp days. Rediffusion days. Kitchener, Sparrow, the invasive rum and Coca Cola days. Herb Alpert's Tijuana Brass days. Wood stove, pitch oil stove days. Dirt oven days. Candle and Coleman gas lamp days. Pee in the *posey* under the bed with the fibre mattress days. River and water fight days. Days of Father soaping Sam, the gentle K9, and keeping a sharp eye on his fast but not so furious boys. Ravine for drinking water days. Tonka bean, mango, orange, chinee tambran, red/yellow cashew days. Radio story days, an overworked lawyer named "Portia" facing life in the morning, an eager ear for "None So Blind" midmorning and a suave "Dr. Paul" trying to solve life's conflicts every evening.

Sometimes, standing in the front yard facing the old family house, bruised and deserted now, one gets the inescapable impression that this monument of loneliness and neglect wants to share her tale before the final onslaught of a slow, irreversible death. Her multiple pillars have weakened and some have shifted alarmingly, under the weight of termite-free mora and other hardwood, rusted zinc sheets and broken, familiar furniture; old books, with such classics as Alexandre Dumas's *Three Musketeers*, Daniel Defoe's *Robinson Crusoe*, Victor Hugo's *Les Misérables* and Miguel de Cervantes' *Don Quixote*. The tall grass in the backyard taunts and chokes the memory of playing marbles for *bokey*, an infliction that left knuckles bruised and swollen, a grim reminder that if you couldn't bear the pain, don't play the game. The green thorny barrier foils any attempt to discern where the soot-stained pitch oil tin, with the boiling ham inside, stood on three rounded stones, the blazing wood warming the heart and hungry stomachs with childish anticipation. Cruel barcano trees wedged their thick trunks, with overtones of sexual indecency, into the widening crevices of the blackened kitchen walls.

I know I will fall soon, the sombre structure moans intuitively, unable to contain the bats that cling to her rafters while others dart around as if performing in a frenzied circus act. I know the end is near, this grand old lady continues, but hear this: they were good days. Father worked hard. Mother loved as a loyal mother should. And argued as a grieved wife would. Children were children. They played, they fought, they had their favourite brother or sister, they went to school by bus, by truck, on foot, in their first grey Peugeot; they went to church on Sundays and usually slept through the Irishman's five a.m. mass. They blessed the luscious bananas bought by six-thirty a.m. in a swirling market where every creed and race jostled for produce in a jubilant atmosphere. They said grace, as faithful Catholics would, over bread, black pudding, watercress, Hong Wing coffee and Sunday newspaper comics.

They were respected by neighbours. They had educational success. They sat down, laughed, ate, rose up, got married and left home.

The dew off the battered eave fell like gentle teardrops. Mother was gone. Seventy-eight years of an animated ancestry hidden from human eyes and aging, fading memories in a quiet Tunapuna plot. Fifty-seven years of marriage proclaimed on an expensive plaque, with dark brown borders and bronze lettering, casually observed by the odd visitor to this incommunicado land of dead bones.

Fast forward.

Father sat in his armchair, his placid eyes riveted on the distant hills. His fingers tightened feebly on the armrest, frantically clutching some support; clutching the web of life that was daily thinning out. It was as though he too was searching for the answer to the very question that confronted his children: 'what should be done with him?' A geriatric home, maybe, but Father always quivered at the thought. That afternoon, Vince, his youngest son, left the family meeting distressed. All doors seemed closed. The choice was his. But could he slam the door on his father? There was talk at that meeting about short-term measures.

"I could have him for a night. On weekends there are business associates to accommodate!" said Robert.

"I for a day," said Grace, the eldest girl. "But I have a beach house in Maracas to look after. It can't be more than a day."

Then, there was the issue of money. Sure, Father had a bank account, but would the salary for a live-in maid, if one could be found, come from his savings?

"What good would a fixed deposit interest be to the old man anyway?" asked Noel, the college principal.

Grace, named as executrix in Father's will, gave him a sharp cut-eye. But money wasn't the problem. A live-in maid would probably work for a week. Who would fill in the weekend? The meeting had tried to settle this burning question. Time was running out. If Father had to be placed in a home, it had to be done by Friday. The meeting made the point: no one was willing to take Father in.

Then Vince did something he feared he would regret: "I'll have him," he said. "Won't we?" He turned to his wife Ruth. She nodded, lips pursed tightly. Did he sense reluctance? What would their children say? Whatever. Father was priority.

Five years ago, Mother was buried. She died at home after a short illness. It was always Father's policy to keep her at home despite the inconveniences and his own limitations. Hospital was taboo. He made her his commitment and it was a commitment sealed with love. After her death, he lamented that her body wasn't brought back home on the day of the funeral. Later, he requested that his body be brought back home for his funeral service instead of being *paraded* in a fancy parlour.

Although Father's once vibrant voice had subsided into a mumbled whisper, his voiced desire continued to echo in Vince's ear. Perhaps he was right in honouring his father's wish. Alright. He had already made his decision. Heavens! Maybe it was a decision veiled with doubt. He felt guilty and confused.

As Vince wrestled with such thoughts, Nyron, an acquaintance, flashed before him. What did it cost Nyron to look after his bed-ridden mother? The answer was clear: he led a life of sacrifice. Nyron's mother, Agnes, was the victim of a spinal disorder and anyone, in that remote neighbourhood, could firmly assert that he was a monument of devotion. He had forfeited many things; his personal life was at stake. Despite the lonely hours that he would face, looking after his mother rekindled the love that bound him to her. Agnes had become his responsibility by choice. Although Nyron's cousin operated a geriatric home, Nyron wouldn't budge: his mother stayed with him.

Vince felt that since he had consented by words he needed some advice to prop him. He turned to Nyron. Nyron agreed it wasn't an easy job but he adamantly stated:

"Senility is a short fuse for an explosive called *neglect*, and, sad enough, neglect is a harsh reality. Looking after Mother hasn't been a bed of roses but I owe it all to her."

For countless nights, Nyron would be awakened by the sobbing of his mother. He would put his feelings in his pocket and try to soothe her. Fear was sometimes the stimulus of her weeping but rest assured she had a hand that she could clutch: a hand held out in love; a hand that would prove true. Nyron would caress her palms and sing to her in the wee hours of the morning until, gradually, she would return to that state of peace.

Although Nyron had dedicated his life to his mother and had little opportunity to venture out and satisfy his human inclinations, he had become a persistent feature in his neighbourhood. Many would flock to him and admire him for cherishing what was his. But Nyron lamented:

"Sad to think they would never have an opportunity to take my example and make it a reality. They're without parents." He pointed to the children's home across the street.

Vince left Nyron with a renewed feeling. In fact, he chuckled at the thought that he now felt invincible. If Nyron could do it for twelve years, maybe he should approach his beginning with more zeal and confidence. He tilled these words in his mind: 'Senility is a short fuse for neglect.' Did he really recognise his father's senility or simply ignored it? How often did he visit Father while a sister cared for him until she herself was overrun by health problems? He turned from the questions.

As he looked at Father's fingers, poised on his chest and touching each other in characteristic pensive fashion, Vince remembered the days when those same fingers wielded a sharp blade through brush and brier. Father always liked the yard around the house clean. He had built the home with hard-earned money he got as department head in a downtown hardware store. 'Clean as a whistle,' he would say. 'And cliché or no cliché, you be sure to have this place spotless when I come around that corner on my bike,' he would warn his boys stentoriously.

Somehow, Vince felt that his brothers feared the old man. In those days, electricity had not come to the few houses scattered in the valley. Cooking was by wood-fire and water was filled by bucket from the stream at the bottom of a steep hill. With each bucketful, the empty oil drum, its inside lined thinly with tar, gurgled mockingly as Vince and his brothers would turn again for the next trek.

But Vince was lucky. He was the last child, the *'bayhee,'* as his brothers would single him out to friends or strangers. It was a French-*patois* word and the mention of it made Vince feel that it was a crime to be the last child in any family. 'You have never tasted Father's belt,' they would tell Vince. 'You don't know about pressure!' They did not fear the old man; he believed some hated him. He suspected, too, that it was only Mother's stoic approach to adversity that kept the family together. Yet Vince was never really terrified of Father. He calculated that if he did nothing wrong and kept out of folly, Father's wrath would not be stirred.

He had to admit, too, as he prepared toast and cheese, Father's favourite, that life was not easy for the old man. Born to a timid village girl and under the care of a man who was a cobbler and not his real parent, Father often felt the weight of a hand strengthened by jealousy and contempt. But time released him from his prison and he moved to the city. When still in his teens, at the invitation of a respectable godfather, he was placed with an English firm. He liked his job and the Englishman liked him. Promoted, it was no financial risk to embark on marriage.

Mother, a descendant of the French Creoles, was charming, aristocratic and a lover of dramatic poetry. The latter, Vince reflected as he went to Father's bedside and propped him up for the meal, was probably responsible for Father's persistent craving for quality reading material. Mother, obviously of cultured background, had won Father's admiration.

Looking at Father chewing awkwardly and noisily on the toast, Vince remembered the evenings when Father would probe through his literary collection, select a neatly papered book, cross his legs and become a character in the adventures of Cervantes' *Don Quixote*. Yet for all this, Father hardly ever read to his children. He was enamoured with Mother and busy with extra work when he joined the Special Reserve Police, climbing to the rank of sergeant.

One day, following a weekend parade, Father came home with a framed photograph. Vince remembered that they had all gathered round him as he nailed the frame to the old wooden partition. Years later, Father would write to a Catholic nun who visited the home: 'The Governor in the photograph chatting with me, seconds after pinning on the Police Long Service Medal award, is the Englishman, Sir Graham.' In that same letter, written to 'confess' and 'admit' that he was guilty of not giving God praise for fifty years of successful marriage, Father could not refrain from sticking in a little of his academic prowess: 'Having eleven children, seven of whom are boys, I took a course in tailoring from the Board of Industry Training and was awarded the Stephen Gold Medal in the intermediate and final exams.'

That evening, and other painful evenings to come, Father was a long way from that gold medal. He lay in bed, feet swollen and heavily powdered to kill any unpleasant odour that would emit from soiled sheets. Father had become unpredictable. He would be tidied one minute and the next, the job could be started all over again. With visitors, came panic.

"Quick! Cover Grandpa!" the children would say, scampering off to his room. "Who wants to confront medicated bedsores? Quick! Replace his false teeth!"

Gradually, however, a routine took shape. Yet, Vince was the one in anguish. Getting Father to the bath was proving too much. Once, as Father slipped to the wet floor, his false teeth snapped dangerously against Vince's shirt. Ruth, meanwhile, would do the laundering but hardly had a *stomach* for personal involvement. Thank God for their eldest daughter, Maria, a monument of patient and pleasant contribution.

Vince kept enduring; Father kept silent; the family hardly put in a meaningful visit.

As he made his rounds through the house one night, Vince suddenly stood still. Father's mumbled prayer drifted across the room:

"Even though I walk through the valley of the shadow of death… I would fear no evil."

The burden weighed heavily on Vince. He was exhausted. Now, more than ever, a geriatric home seemed the only recourse. His mind was fixed: he couldn't cope any longer as Father's health zeroed. The naked reality eventually reached everyone; but no one seemed really affected.

Father was moved to a *home*. Finance wasn't the problem that faced the family but a lack of togetherness; a vacuum existed in terms of love. Gradually, Father lost his will to live. He felt locked out from the world and looked into a gulf of solitude. These pangs of depression seemed to intensify his senility. Daily he would weep, but his children were too busy. He didn't even have his familiar old chair to squeeze. Now, with such intense pain, he might not just grip it, but dig his nails through the sponge. It wasn't long before this emotional trauma subsided. One afternoon, amidst lonely silence, he breathed the fatal breath.

The organ sounded. *Six* sons carried the casket to the top of the aisle. Relatives filed into the front pews. Outside, the hearse was overflowing with wreaths. This was the funeral parade that Father felt he could have done without. Noel read the eulogy:

"He gave us one gift: he loved our mother and he loved us."

Vince walked out of the Catholic Church with Nyron at his side. The clergyman's words haunted him:

"Beautiful wreaths make a beautiful send-off. But remember: give them the flowers when they are alive."

Somehow, Vince felt he had failed.

Rat

Rat made a living walking around Trincity with a bag on his back, asking residents for small change and eats, anything at all: a twen'y dollar bill, a plate of food, tins of sardine, soda in cans or if they couldn't spare a twen'y, eleven-dollars-and-thirty-five-cents so he could buy a loaf of bread. After two months on the job he knew the streets with the bad dogs, the dead ends and makeshift bridges to other avenues. He avoided blocks the pushers worked (when his cravings got the better of him he purchased crack in Arouca, a town two miles away, because he didn't believe in messing on his doorstep). He knew the residents who worked shift, who gave money versus a meal and who invited him inside their gallery for a plate of food and a drink and still gave him money for a loaf of bread.

Today, Rat hurried towards the Lopez's residence because it was three days before Christmas and he needed money and food. In military boots, cargo pants and a beret, he looked like a hard times suicide bomber. He hobbled with his neck craned forward like an ostrich, walking with a limp an Alsatian had given him after it ripped a junk of flesh from his calf but, of course, Rat told his Indian sympathisers that had happened way back when he worked as a K9 trainer for a security firm that slumped and eventually crashed under the reinstated government, those black, thieving sons-of-bitches; Africans heard a slightly modified version of the same story; and mixed folks had to listen to a stomach-churning tale that involved a Chinese restaurant and a Chiwawa.

It was four-thirty when Rat turned into a street lined with concrete flats and fenced yards dotted with mango trees and bougainvillea hedges. On either side, all the way to the end of the street, patches of lawn poked out of the pavement. Two houses down, Emmanuel Lopez had just parked his truck on the pavement in front his house and was on the tray stacking pallets. Across the road the front gate was open and Dexter, Lopez's neighbour, was drying his car with a t-shirt. When he saw Rat, he straightened and glared and wrung the t-shirt as if he wished it were Rat's neck; Rat casually raised his middle finger, mouthed an expletive and slid between the truck and spiked fence as Emmanuel lifted a blue tarpaulin to his chest and threw it over the rails and into his yard with a tired grunt.

"It is Wednesday," Rat said, surprising Emmanuel. "You're home half-an-hour late."

Emmanuel climbed over the truck rails and onto the spiked fence then jumped down into his yard. Suddenly, an Alsatian craned its head around the side of the house then bounded across the garage towards Emmanuel. Stroking the dog, Emmanuel said, "I'm home late because my truck got a flat."

Shaking his head, Rat sighed. "That happened to a good man like you?" He made a clicking noise in his throat and when the Alsatian went up on its hind legs and rested its front paws against the fence, he pushed his hands through and encouraged the dog to lick them. "Did you get the flat on your way to or from Point Fortin?"

"Come here, Tom," Emmanuel said, but the dog didn't respond. Frowning, Emmanuel folded his lips inwards and squatted before the tarpaulin. "That's funny. He doesn't usually take to strangers."

Rat smiled. "Tom knows that you and I are friends."

"Yes, that's true."

"On another note," Rat said and stopped smiling, "spare me a twen'y?"

Emmanuel had lifted the tarpaulin to his shoulder. He used one hand to balance his load and with the other he overturned his pockets. "Today isn't a good day, my friend."

Rat interlaced his fingers, dipped his head and stared at the ground, as if wishing it would swallow him. "Anything at all? Twen'y dollars will go a long way." He waved as if to say *fo'get it.*

Emmanuel smiled lamely. I should fetch my wallet, he thought, but what good would it do, for I really am as broken as a thief. After an awkward silence, Emmanuel excused himself and went to the annex in the backyard where he stored the tarpaulin. While he was away, Rat grabbed and squeezed Tom's muzzle so viciously that the dog lurched back and barked and didn't stop, not even when Emmanuel swiftly reappeared or his wife stuck her head through the kitchen window and exclaimed, "Shush Tom!"

"Mrs. Lopez," Rat hollered, sliding along the space between the fence and truck until he came to the front gate. "How are you today? How is the season treating you? What are your plans this Christmas?"

"Oh," Mrs. Lopez exclaimed as Emmanuel collared Tom and led him, still barking, to the backyard. "We're visiting family in Icacos this weekend."

"Really?" Rat clutched the gate, squeezed his face through and peered at Mrs. Lopez, who wore a green button-front duster. "I'm originally from Icacos. What's your maiden name?"

Emmanuel had returned. He unlocked an entrance built into the main gate and let Rat in.

"I'm a Cozier," she said, as Rat walked up the garage, taking off his bag. He and Emmanuel sat on a mission bench below the kitchen window, facing each other so that the window was between them and it was easy to converse with Mrs. Lopez inside. There were two metal pots on the stove. The kitchen smelled of cloves and sweet mustard because there was a ham in the oven.

Pinching his nose, Rat frowned. "*Panther* and *Pounce* is your brothers?"

Mrs. Lopez laughed. "Yes, those are my younger brothers."

"Shit, boy, you re'l resemble them." Rat squinted. "Which sister are you?"

"Estavia."

Repeating the name, Rat rubbed behind his head. "You mean *Pooksie*?"

"That's me!" Mrs. Lopez exclaimed.

"Cozier, girl," Rat said, removing his beret, "I is Ramdhanie's son, the las' one."

"Wait, Boysie, is you?" Mrs. Lopez put her hands on the counter and stuck her head further out the window. "How you end up–"

"Something's burning," Emmanuel interjected. Mrs. Lopez disappeared and the noise of a metal spoon knocking against ceramic filtered through the window.

Shaking his head, Rat slapped Emmanuel on his shoulder and said something about all this time he'd been visiting and he didn't know he was *family*. "You mean to tell me that Cozier is *your* wife?" Rat laughed, scornfully, agitating Emmanuel. Thumping his heart, Rat continued, "Cozier is blood, boy! Father! She wasn't easy y'u know? Yeah. Plenty fellars did like she in she young days. Now look at her, living in a big shot area."

Mrs. Lopez reappeared, muttered something to Emmanuel and passed two ceramic plates with hot rice, lentil peas and stewed turkey through the window. "Did you ask Dexter about Tom?"

"Yes, he agreed to feed him while we are away."

"Cozier," Rat snickered, "you still looking good. You sure you is not Emmanuel's daughter?"

Mrs. Lopez crossed her arms; Emmanuel frowned at the grinning man. Before excusing herself, she placed two glasses of pink grapefruit juice (dashed with Angostura Bitters, spreading slowly, like ink in water) and two tins of sardine on the counter for Rat to take away. Tom was still barking in the backyard. Rat scooped his rice to one side, ate the peas and turkey then, without asking, stuck his hand in Emmanuel's plate and took his meat. He ignored or didn't notice Emmanuel's glance of disapproval and that Tom had stopped barking, so, moving without any break in his rhythm, he limped to the backyard, scraped the rice and mangled bones for Tom and when he was certain that the dog had eaten, he returned to the garage, drank the two glasses of now dark-pink grapefruit juice, secured the two tins of sardine in his shirt pocket and heaved his bag over his shoulder.

"I will need bread," he said to Emmanuel, who had quit eating and rested his plate on the bench. "I need eleven-dollars-and-thirty-five-cents."

"Rat, what the heck is wrong with you?" Emmanuel growled and in the backyard, Tom's barking resumed. "I already told you that I have no money. Look! You see this begging! Don't come back here for a while. And I don't care if you know all the Coziers from Trinidad to St. Vincent."

Smirking, shrugging and pointing between his boots and Emmanuel's buttocks, Rat refused to leave the yard, but when Dexter stopped polishing his car and crossed the road, wringing a jockey shorts as if it were Rat's neck, his smile disappeared and he hobbled away muttering darkness. At the end of the street, he slipped into a paved drain, as deep as a grave and too wide to jump. Inside the drain, the ground sloped downwards to a mossy channel in the centre. The water was brown, shallow and fast-flowing and its scalloped edges licked at the walls. Concentrating on keeping his boots clean, Rat hugged the wall and walked south until he came to a bridge the drain flowed beneath. Overhead, vehicles zipped along the highway.

Rat lived in a camp below the bridge, a rumbling concrete expanse decorated with paint buckets, rabbit grass and every-day trash. The walls were adorned with handprints slapped on with yellow paint and the words *"Rat is my name"* written in charcoal. In his "backyard" the drain emptied into a stagnant pool that disappeared between sugarcane stalks. When Rat was out working he left behind a hard times dog named *Jerry XII* to guard the camp because of a curious alligator that lived in the area. The dog was tied to a pram and asleep on a wooden pallet Rat used as a bed. Cussing, he removed his belt and beat the dog until it couldn't walk and then until it couldn't whine. After Rat composed himself, he drowned *Jerry XII* in the pool out back.

Ten minutes before sunset, Rat spread cardboard and sponge on two wooden pallets and covered his bed with a sheet he kept in his bag. Whistling, he removed a switchblade from his waist and a can of soda from his cargo pants then he popped the soda and shook out the contents. Using his thumbs, he squeezed the can along the length of its body creating a sort of mutilated *bowl*. Next, he pricked tiny air holes in the bowl then he bored a *carb* hole closer to the mouth of the can and widened it by dancing his knife in a circle. Gingerly, Rat removed a piece of foil wrapped into a tight ball from his boots. He peeled it back revealing a beautiful white rock the size of a pebble which he admired between his thumb and forefinger. He placed the rock on his soda can *pipe*. Holding a flame to the rock, he smoked through the mouth of the can, got high and after a bout of karate with an alligator armed with nun chucks, he went to bed. Around two o'clock in the morning, long after his high had worn off, he realised he was out of coke so he screamed until daybreak.

Rat prised open the two tins of sardine Mrs. Lopez had given him, sat on his bed like a yogi, ate all of one then he placed the *opened, untouched* tin in a hole in the wall and left it to rot, while he hobbled around the settlement west of the drain soliciting. Although it was Christmas Eve and Savannah Drive residents milled around their front lawns, talking hard, laughing loud and drinking scotch and coconut water, Rat didn't make any money, so he went home bitter and sober.

Christmas night, scratching his neck, arms and face non-stop, Rat removed the sardine tin from the hole in the wall and, hiding it behind his back, walked to the Lopez residence. The curtains were pulled, the house in darkness. Tom, the Alsatian, wasn't around. Rat quickly squeezed between the truck and fence and shuffled towards the tray where he secured the sardine. He tossed his bag in the yard, climbed on the truck's rear tyre and hopped over the fence. No cause for alarm, he retrieved the sardine, scurried along the side of the house, shielding his face from an ixora hedge, and circled to the back. Tom was lying in his kennel, untied. The gate was open. Rat made a clicking noise in his throat and Tom stood and pounced at him, playfully.

Rat squatted and, stroking Tom, whispered, "I have something nice for you." He placed the sardine tin on the ground and Tom dug in, because Dexter hadn't fed him since Mr. and Mrs. Lopez left for the weekend. Minutes later, Tom, foaming at his mouth and snarling, dashed around the house three or four times then dropped dead.

Rat snickered and turned his attention to the house. The back door was locked but the window in the middle room proved a sight for shifty eyes: louvers. Once inside, Rat went to the master bedroom. He turned on a light and a ceiling fan, set down his bag, jumped on the bed and rolled around with his boots on. In the kitchen, he opened the refrigerator and a light came on revealing a ham wrapped in foil, a turkey minus a leg in a glass platter, lettuce in an ice-cream container filled with water, a bowl of stuffing wrapped in plastic and condiments. Rat left the refrigerator door open and glanced around: there was a bag of hops-bread on top the microwave and a knife downturned in the wares rack beside the sink.

Smiling, he adjusted his beret and went to work, not knowing that across the road, Dexter had observed his silhouette moving around the kitchen and dialled 999.

Rat was on his eighth sandwich when the cops showed. Panicking, he dashed for the side door, but wheeled around when he glimpsed three, armed officers hustling towards him. He would never make it to the window in the middle room, he reasoned, and a familiar voice chasing him through the narrow corridors terrified him, so he dove facedown beneath the bed in the master bedroom and covered his head with a pillow that had fallen.

Officer Thomas entered the room with his gun drawn. He peeked beneath the bed. "Peek-a-boo! A-a! Mr. Boysie Ramdhanie, is that you?"

"Yes, officer," Rat stuttered, "bu' I not t'iefing."

"Rat, listen, speak the truth, what are you doing in this house?"

"I babysitting the place," Rat stuttered. "Me and the Coziers go way back. They leave a key under the mat fo' me."

Thomas sighed. "So why did you enter through the back window?"

"Dread, officer," Rat reasoned, "I los' the key."

"Dread? Who are you calling dread, *dread?*" Thomas barked. "Why are you under the bed?"

Rat said, "I thought all y'u was bandits!"

Officer Boodram entered the master bedroom with his gun drawn. "The other rooms clear. Where the lil bugger?"

"Under the bed," Thomas said. "It's Boysie Ramdhanie."

Boodram jerked his head backwards. "Boysie who?"

"Rat from Arouca," Thomas said.

"You mean to say that bitch ain't learn he lesson?" Boodram kneeled on the other side of the bed so that Rat was trapped between the two officers. "Wha's tha' in you' hand, Rat, a knife? Wha' you was going to do, stab we?"

Rat wiggled away from Boodram. "Nah, I was cutting ham, I swear." He looked at the knife then slid it across the tiles to Officer Thomas.

When someone knocked on the back door, Boodram stood and opened it. Officer Ali entered holding the sardine tin Rat had set for Tom.

"There's a dead German Shepherd in the backyard," he said. "Where's the son-of-a-bitch?"

"Is Rat," Boodram said. "He below the bed."

Ali kneeled where Boodram had been and raised the bed sheet. He spoke comfortably to Rat. "You have a choice," he said, "we can shoot you in your legs or you can eat the rest of this sardine."

"No-no-no!" Rat cried, jerking closer to Thomas and kicking up dust beneath the bed; when Thomas sneezed three times, he said, "Bless you, officer."

"Boodram," Thomas said, "when we caught Rat in that house in Arouca, which leg did I shoot him in?"

Boodram scratched below his chin with his gun's barrel. "Behind he left foot."

"We really should shoot him again," Thomas suggested.

"Or make him eat the rest of this sardine," Ali added.

Rat was crying and scampering below the bed, closer to Officer Thomas one second, up under Officer Ali the other. "All y'u cyar shoot me in here," he cried. "Mr. and Mrs. Lopez does sleep in this bedroom."

Thomas sighed. "You should have thought about that before you broke in."

"The choice is yours, Rat," Ali said, and slid the sardine tin under the bed. "Which one is it? The sardine or a bullet in each leg?"

Rat's sobbing escalated into what sounded like hysterical laughter, and, begging for compassion, he spread his legs, slowly, like a rookie gymnast on his stomach attempting a split, so that his legs poked out from either side of the bed. Thomas and Ali pressed their guns into Rat's legs. Boodram went to the bed head and rested his foot on Rat's skull.

"Rat, relax y'u'self," he said. "Next time, think before you thief."

When Rat agreed, Thomas and Ali simultaneously fired, blowing tissue away.

Nine months later, on a Wednesday, at four-thirty in the afternoon, Rat, a free man, found himself on the street the Lopez family lived on. The truck was parked on the pavement with the side rails lowered. Emmanuel was on the tray, rolling empty oil drums from the front to the back. Mrs. Lopez was in the front yard watering the lawn with a hose. When she noticed Rat, she shook her head and led an Alsatian pup lying beside her to the backyard. Rat paused, bag on back, loot in sack, and although not a reformed man, apology crossed his mind, but not his heart. Emmanuel stooped, put one hand on the tray and jumped down to the road. He beckoned Rat closer.

"Mr. Lopez," Rat said, like an egoistic doctor of science, "not me and tha' shit again, y'u know, not me and tha' shit, I'm a reformed man."

With his eyebrows lowered, Emmanuel pursed his lips and nodded, not looking into Rat's eyes, but at his forehead.

"I mean," Rat continued, "only today I was passing by a car and the doors were open and there was a cell phone on the driver's seat, I didn't take it, it never even crossed my mind." Emmanuel stopped nodding after Rat said, "I mean, after all, these telephone companies have GPS systems, it wouldn't be hard for them to trace me, wouldn't be hard at all. On another note, spare me a twen'y?"

Emmanuel emptied his pockets, gave Rat eleven-dollars-and-thirty-five-cents and said, low and slow, "Rat, it's 'bout time you moved out of this town."

That night, Rat stole the Lopez's Alsatian pup and limped to the hills overlooking El Dorado. When his cravings got the better of him, he left *Jerry XIII* to guard his camp and visited the pushers in Trincity.

Lounge act

The broad sat footsteps from me. I've always been a sucker for redheads and hers curled just the way I liked it, decorating her shoulders and giving me sneak peeks of her breasts, hidden behind a red dress with a taunting slit that revealed the legs of an exercised woman. She sat there, legs crossed, smoking pencillong cigarettes that never seemed to burn out. Each puff floated my way and intoxicated me further. From the separating distance, I whiffed the perfume she wore and I was reminded of Mrs. Lovell, my primary school crush.

Thick smoke hung around the redhead, giving her the glamour rock bands get each time they make a grand appearance, as she waved off a few sober losers and brave drunks. They would leave, a few inches shorter, but generally their shattered egos went unnoticed by people lounging with merry company. It was obvious she was waiting on someone, rather patiently I might add, and it was time for me to find new, redheaded blood. I took a drink from an already emptied glass.

I ordered another drink from over my shoulder and from the far end of the teak counter, the barman slid a Scotch on the Rocks towards me. I rotated clockwise just in time to grab the drink and felt the chill of the glass in my palms. The bouquet of perfume had grown stronger. There she is behind you, the mirror indicated.

Her hands caressed my back. I turned, moved to speak but an index finger covered my lips. She is soft, but her touch firm and groping. Bedroom eyes. She nibbled my ear, raising the pores on my neck. Sweet, smooth, flirtatious voice. Radio voice. I do not know you, she whispers, but I want to, it is my will, let it be done in ten minutes sharp; the restroom. Then suddenly she left.

Ten minutes ticked by slowly. I rose but stumbled. I did not find her in the restroom. The ladies' was empty as well. Disheartened, I returned to the bar and downed five more drinks of whiskey ever hoping for her reflection, which never materialised. It is not tradition, but I drank until closing time. When the barman signalled *no more*, I reached for my wallet but it was gone.

The cycle

The first time it happened, the drama unfolded like this:

"Boy, humph, I have something to tell you."

"What's that, my girl?"

"I will tell you later."

I get blue vex one time. The worst thing a woman could do is tell you that she has something important to say, but she will tell you later. Is at tha' very moment man does get re'l testy and defensive. The faithful fellow does be wondering if he left the toilet seat up at home, if he forget to take out garbage or if the woman suspect he conducting extra curricula activities. The player, on the other hand, does ge' on rowdy. I is not the latter, so I pull the car on the shoulder and give my girl a questioning look.

"Well, what is the matter?" I calmly ask because I love my girl a lot.

"You sure you want to know?" She biting her lip and watching me, but is not a look like she want to make love; is more like she worried about what I go think. "You sure you ready to be a father?"

I shake my head. Then it register. "Wait, wha' you saying?"

"Yes, I think I'm pregnant. My period skipped, and you know I'm never late."

Pressure! I hold on to the steering wheel and start to bawl like a cow that giving birth to a elephant. I shake up the steering wheel, I bang my head on it, I pump the horn, I shake up the whole car. When I done, my face and ears red. Next thing I hear somebody knocking on the window. When I look is a police man.

"What you doing making love on the side of the highway?" he ask, when I wind down the window. "The whole car shaking up." He give me a ticket and leave.

I start to bawl again. My blood pressure raise until I get a pain in the back of my neck. "You sure, babe?" I watching she belly, wishing I had x-ray vision.

"Yeah my period a week late."

It was a question not a statement: "That not good?"

"I don't know *nah*," she say, bumping her fingertips together.

I whisper a prayer. "Don't worry, seven days is not that bad. It just late, don't worry." I said it for myself more than for her.

Two weeks later, my girl period ain't come as yet. During this time, I lose all appetite for love, food and sex. Every time my cell phone ring, I hoping is my girl calling with some good news, but no luck. I wouldn't lie, after I find out about the symptoms of pregnancy, I start to get some wicked cramps and cravings for green mango, salt and pepper. I study how my parents would put me out; plus my money wasn't reading right. I was nowhere near ready to be a father.

My girl called Friday night. "My breasts are feeling sore."

"One or two of them?"

"I think is the right one. Let me check. No. Both of them."

I hung up.

Saturday morning, bright and early, I hustle to the pharmacy and ask for three different brands of pregnancy test. Honestly, I was expecting a user manual, but all I get was three plastic packs, about the length of pencils, and a piece of paper with three diagrams. Each diagram was a rectangle with the labels C and T. A solid line next to the C meant negative, T was positive, or *trouble* as the pharmacist joked, and any combination of the two was an invalid result.

When I returned home, my girl was there, sitting on a stool, knocking her knees together and massaging her eyebrows vigorously. "You get the thing?" My girl wasn't as anxious as I was. If she was, she was hiding it good.

"Right here," I say, handing her two. I open the third test and out popped a rectangular, white, hard plastic contraption.

"What C for?" she asked. "Condom?"

I laugh. "No. That means things cool."

"And the T? Trouble?"

I nodded. "A bellyful!" I indicated a pin-sized hole at the base. "You have to get four drops of pee here."

"How I doing that?" she squealed.

After prolonged mutual confusion, I checked the package. There was a small plastic dropper inside. "You will need a cup." I grabbed one from the kitchen.

"That is not your mother good glass?"

"Small thing. We will wash it after."

My girl went inside the bathroom. I waited on the couch in the living room. There is a suspended stillness which I must alert the inexperienced boy or man to whom this scenario is unfamiliar. It is a dreadful calm, not the serene, reassuring one of a holy place, such as a church or in a temple, neither is it the gloomy sadness one feels the night after a burial. It is the hollow, gut-wrenching second before a bus slams into you – over and over again.

Chill screams erupted from the bathroom, ones capable of loosening bowels. I ran towards her.

"What happen, girl?"

"I pregnant!" she squealed.

I grabbed the wet test from her. The *trouble* line was solid and the *cool* halfway-filled.

"Girl, you crazy or what?" I more nervous than angry at the commotion. "That mean it invalid. Try again."

"I don't have any more pee," she confessed. "I throw it away."

If I wasn't anxious I would have been angry. In thirty minutes, I pour my girl ten glasses of water. She disappeared into the bathroom again. Five minutes later, she reappeared smiling.

"Everything cool," she boasted. True to form, the C line solid in both tests.

"Well, le' we doh count we eggs before they hatch. I go only be happy when your periods come."

It come tha' same night. I hug up myself and laugh. I feel in love all over again. I went in the kitchen and eat a bag of Crix and a bottle of jam. I drink some oysters in *chando beni* sauce that it had in the fridge. That night I lay awake for a long time, thinking rudeness. I call my girl about two in the morning and tell her how I wanted to make out: she said, no problem, as long as I didn't use a condom, because she was my girl and she wanted to feel re'l sweet too.

Bottles made in Trinidad

The pockets of foreign chatter ceased when the ferry's engines laboured into reverse. There was an abrasive shout from the bridge and two sailors with ruddy complexions rushed on deck. One skipped to the bow, the other to the stern, and with deft precision they tossed heaving lines to hands on the jetty. The vessel moored with the little dignity and grace left in her. Passengers stood and began gathering their luggage despite the captain's command to remain seated. The engines were cut. The passengers erupted in half-hearted applause; someone, I didn't see who, exclaimed, 'Madre de dios!' There was laughter but it was insecure. Disquiet soon turned to agitation as the crew floundered in establishing the gangway.

I had returned to Trinidad after three hours of terror on an ash grey sea, and I hustled from the ferry with such anxiety I managed to secure the wrath of a mother fussing over three children, and the professional suspicion of a customs officer, with unforgettable ears and an enormous stomach, waiting behind a white, peeling podium placed on the pier without shade. Without pleasantries, he requested my documents and glanced between my smiling passport and solemn face as if they were not one and the same.

"Rose *Constantine*," he said. His brows furrowed. "Are you related to *the* Constantine?"

"I am."

He regarded my filthiness and sad slippers with obvious doubt, smirked and, indicating to two pink suitcases smudged with mud and standing beside me, enquired, "Those are yours?"

"They are," I replied, observing his height increase and his chest bloat, for I knew he desired to interrogate me until offered a small bribe.

"You did a lot of Christmas shopping?"

"I have not."

"You *have not?*" he stuttered. "And your bags so full up?"

My temperature rose, but my tone didn't waver, "I had no time to."

"This is absurd," he stammered with pulsating lips. "Explain yourself!"

I began relating my story, intending to spare no detail:

"Having left Trinidad and arrived in Venezuela *yesterday* after incessant prayers for a safe journey, I met my companion whom I recognised by a photograph she had posted to father. She was waiting on the docks in the sweltering midday heat, dressed in poor, thick clothes that stuck to her skin, and armed with combed yet unruly hair the colour of soot. I cleared Customs with great difficulty, being uncultured in *everyday* Spanish and having in my possession these same two, pink suitcases, stuffed like monsters, which made the officer regard me with the same distrust. Unlike you, however, when he finally understood that I only had personal items, he let me through. Finally, coming upon the woman, I wondered aloud:

"'Aunty Marta Flores?'

"'Rose Constantine?' she queried – her rolling accent confirmed I was in a foreign land – but before I could reassert my position, she manacled my shoulders, thrust her breasts against my face and planted four, sweaty kisses upon me, two on either cheek. She held me at arm's length, regarded my tenuous attire and high heels with scepticism and exclaimed without conviction, 'Bienvenida a Venezuela!'

"'Bienvenido!' I replied.

"Aunty Marta Flores laughed off my Spanish blunder. 'Trinidad!' she said, pointing to the choppy December ocean.

"In the sea there were thousands of melancholy bottles, labelled by Trinidadian manufacturers, nudging each other; as far as the eye could see; beneath the jetty leading to the terminal; all the way along the coast; even beyond the rocks, shooting into the sea and leading to a solitary lighthouse where faceless persons, large and small, were sitting with knees propped up to their chests, some smoking, some talking, some tugging fishing lines tucked between thumb and forefinger.

"(At this point the customs officer, this is the one in Trinidad to whom I was relating my story, interjected: "Wait! The tide takes bottles from Trinidad all the way to Guiria?" But my palms indicated that he mustn't interrupt me again.)

"Yes, the bottles in the water were made in Trinidad. So, we began our journey after Aunty Marta reclaimed the photograph she had sent in the mail; it was a romantic picture of her and my uncle. The maritime town is smaller and sadder than Chaguaramas; its poverty strikes you without forewarning yet most faces are content and round as if well fed. The recent mudslides and floods had devastated the place and blanched the citizens who trudged the narrow streets as if they were slaves being dragged by invisible chains. What struck me, though, was the absence of Latin music and dance; not even a tragic, ornate tune sung in bass was audible. Interesting too were all the abandoned fishing boats, pelicans and seagulls. All the streets seem to slope upwards and the houses are close, like they are in Highgate Avenue, London, but the redbrick buildings are oppressive and lean against each other like old people needing support. I was horrified not only by the thought of armed robbers – for crooks are everywhere: England, America, Trinidad, you name it – but by the bizarre idea the squalid shacks would topple upon me like dominoes. Mother is infected by the absurd idea that the 'communist regime' has supplied even the tiniest tot with a gun and, perhaps, thinking about it now, she is right; there is a sad, dangerous confidence of folk in Guiria. The roads are bumpy too as if paved by an ignorant engineer and patched with mud by a bad plastic surgeon. Burdened faces peered from beyond shadowed doorways, bending upon me glances of suspicion and fleeting amusement. Groups of plagued dogs ambled through the muddy streets as if on roller skates, gnashing vampire teeth at our heels as they passed.

"There is a lot of Trinidadian influence in Guiria with one exception: there are more bicycles than cars. I was amused to see a woman riding a piece of junk made with parts from various models. The vegetation is the same, yet I never saw a mango tree. I might be mistaken but I thought I heard calypso as I passed a restaurant, smelling of cornmeal and fried pork. One barebacked boy who saw me struggling with this same pink luggage shouted as if it were a term of endearment, 'Coolie!'

"Marta Flores was short but she walked with quick, long strides, trundling one of my pink pieces without care or caution. She did this without gazing left or right but my inclination was to stop and grieve at the wounded hills that had wept mud days ago. She never stopped except when a peculiar man with eyes like a goldfish, propped on a three-legged chair before a store, saluted her with infantile enthusiasm. Otherwise, she walked the rising streets with flat shoes and hunched shoulders, submerged in fathomless thought.

"Marta Flores had had the misfortune of being once married to my wayward but jovial uncle. He had brought her to Trinidad during my university years in London and although the pleasure had never been mine, she and my parents established a cordial relationship, communicating through photographs, gestures and exasperated outbursts which sparked laughter. Mother opened the door for Marta Flores when she appeared unannounced in January with black bags below her eyes and a letter dictating in a crooked pen:

"'*Antonio run away to Columbia with a nice white nineteen-year-old thing.*'

"She spent the night in quiet consultation with father, who you very well know to be a prominent Pentecostal pastor. He knows little Spanish – enough not to starve – but, as you well know, he knows the bible from cover to cover and has an impulse for proverbial quips. We never saw Marta Flores again but we did receive a note in early December, only days ago, written with the same urgent hand that had reported my uncle's adultery:

"'*House ruined by flood and mucho mud. Send help! Por favor!*'

"Enclosed in the envelope was a photograph of Aunty Marta Flores.

"'I shall send the first person who enters this room,' father resolved and to mother's dismay I strayed into the kitchen, having just arrived home from London as a wintry surprise.

"Marta Flores's house was at the peak of a hill twenty minutes away from the pier, a colonial mansion with white-washed walls, two storeys high, guarded by high unpainted walls which were broken to the south. The yard was capacious but decimated like the port and fat with mud. Aunty Marta traversed the soft earth, skipping among stones placed for the exact purpose but sensing my hesitation she beckoned me toward her. The earth swallowed my shoes but had no appetite for my suitcase, choosing instead to lick it. However, the magnitude and impossibility of the cleaning campaign I had been summoned to Guiria for never occurred to me.

"Evinrude's strong, chiselled arms saved me from the mud. Who's he? He's one my aunt's tenants. After climbing to the second floor and securing my luggage, after I had found a pair of slippers in my bags, he hustled me downstairs with such childish anxiety I gushed as if we were lovers. The rooms downstairs, eight in all, are built around a courtyard packed with brown slush, dingy chairs and broken pots. Eight arches form a corridor which separates the quadrangle from the rooms.

"'My motorbike,' Evinrude said in shaky English, indicating a red, attractive motorcycle poised on a stand.

"'Do you speak English?' I enquired.

"'Sí,' he replied and liking my smile, 'You are v-e-r-y beau-ti-ful – cómo se dice negra? Ah sí – you are v-e-r-y beau-ti-ful black girl.'

"My response would have been unfavourable hadn't a child's cry unsettled me. Evinrude snatched my left arm and led me along the corridor to the noise. Three filthy children with sticks for limbs greeted my eyes. How horrible, I thought.

"'Señor,' Evinrude mumbled to a man whom I figured he wished not to encounter. The man was squatting, and hunched over a two-burner gas stove propping up a shallow frying pan and a deep ancient pot filled to the brim with black beans bursting with angry bubbles. He wore magenta pants and had a yellow jersey tossed over his shoulder. The man was smoking and stirring the pot with a wooden spoon and long, thoughtful observation. Adjacent to the stove was a low wooden stool. On top it was a handle-less strainer covered with an overturned plate, a box of matches and an opened, quasi-empty pack of Belmont cigarettes. Smoking and cooking! In the corridor of all places! Can you believe it? His wife, a yellowish woman with freckles and blank eyes, cracked the door behind him and scrutinised me without expression. The cook looked up after saying something to his wife; it must have been a command for she disappeared. He had hair like liquid silver, the pronounced nose and narrow jaw of a carica-ture and sharp eyes which softened when he set gaze upon me. He shot to his feet, flicked the fag-end of his cigarette into the courtyard and, apologising without ceasing, donned his cotton top, containing more holes than cloth. In another moment the cooking spoon had been switched to his left hand, his right palm had been rubbed clean against his trou-sers and extending it, he said in a deep, slow voice, calling to my mind the romanticism of Columbian poetry:

"'Señorita, lo siento. Me llamo Señor Simón Vasquez.'

"'Me llamo Rose Constantine,' I said. I was relieved to understand someone – even the dogs bark funny and resist the sucking catcalls Trinidadians use.

"Evinrude excused himself when Señor Simón Vasquez turned iron eyes upon him. 'Jose! Carmen! Pedro!' the cook shouted and his children arranged themselves in tandem from eldest to youngest and one-by-one we shook hands. His wife was Renee and her handshake was feeble and cold, not in manner but to the sense of touch, as if she had been working with ice. She disappeared after the introduction, returning two minutes later with a reed chair I accepted with a silent thank you and placed a safe distance from the fire; but I remained standing. Señor Simón Vasquez spoke without pause, shaking his head at the news of crime and callow politics which I was reluctant to speak of because such talk wearies me. He exclaimed when I mentioned the impending battle between Mexico and the Soca Warriors but I failed to communicate in Spanish why the title had been given to the football squad. In fact I cannot even describe it in my native tongue.

"'Ah Mexico!' he announced and prattled something.

"A man appeared. It was the peculiar soul who had acknowledged Aunty Marta Flores on the streets, the man with eyes like a goldfish. Argenis was his name and he was unusual to say the least; a bit like *Mad Rambo* who walks along the white lines on Trinidad's roads but with a less fuzzy brain. Like Señor Vasquez had been he was barebacked and his right hand was holding up far oversized trousers at the crotch. On seeing him the cook dismissed him with a hostile wave.

"The cook and I spoke at length. I listened hard, learned little, but established that four of the eight rooms were occupied. Señor Vasquez spoke of the upper floor my aunt occupied like it was an impossible dream and it was because he had never been there. When the black beans were finished he began frying plantains in the shallow pan filled with stale oil decorated with tiny, black specks like broken bat wings. From time to time Señor Vasquez stood, sidestepped to another location and stooped again as if trying to shield the wind with his back but there was no breeze. The heat was embracing and atrocious, I daresay worse than London's summer. When the eight yellow slices of plantain had been charred black, he stuck them through with the overturned tines of a fork and, one by one, dished them into the handle-less strainer which to my surprise was filled with steaming rice. He stood and invited me inside for lunch. I declined, perhaps, with an air of alacrity for the Señor inspected me and after an awkward moment smiled at his poverty. 'Jose! Carmen! Pedro!' he shouted and the brown children scurried inside. 'Mucho gusto,' said he and with one last look, he stepped from the corridor into his apartment.

"Evinrude reappeared in the corridor. I accepted the invitation into his apartment without hesitation or fear of reproach for I was an errant guest in a strange land and away from my parents. There was a modern laptop on the bed, a red beret on the pillow and scores of compact discs stacked to the ceiling in one corner like coins. I was dismayed by the closeness of the walls, its peeling paint and the craggy layer of mud on the ground.

"'Does Señor Simón Vasquez live with his wife and three children in a room this tiny?' I asked.

"Evinrude searched for the words and said in English, 'He is a baker.'

"'And Argenis?'

"'Esta loco,' Evinrude hissed, a whirling forefinger at his ear. 'As child he have meningitis.'

(At this point, I paused and looked at the customs officer for I expected him to be weary but he prompted me to continue despite the swelling contention in the passengers standing behind me.)

"My name bouncing around in the courtyard alarmed me.

"'It is my aunt!' I exclaimed, turning to leave but Evinrude's hand and amorous eyes stopped my heart.

"He whispered in perfect English, 'Coolie, I will knock on your window at three o'clock in the morning.'

"My aunt, the landlady, to my delight, occupied the entire upstairs floor, not capacious but comfortable and decorated with a meticulous eye for old Spanish artwork. There was no music. The staircase led to the kitchen where two windows opened into the sea and the town, idyllic in the distance. The sky was a cloudless blue but the ocean grey with silt stretching one mile out from the shore. The kitchen opened into a terrace, paved with red bricks and occupied by two iron chairs, a matching table and four shallow-potted plants in either corner. Aunty Marta warned me to stay shy of the unsteady guard rail; yet I thought of Evinrude as I walked towards the bedrooms in the eastern minaret. There were two bedrooms, the first being the largest and prepared for my coming. Aunty Marta paused in the corridor before a wooden door barred with a jumbo latch and, massaging her skull with ten fingers that looked like white spider legs, exclaimed:

"'El baño!'

"After the tour I ventured to the terrace without changing, and seeing Evinrude, I curtsied and sat. It never occurred I should telephone my parents. He smiled and with five, fluttering fingers dipped into his chest, extracted his heart and tossed it up where it landed in safe hands.

"'Evinrude!' Aunty Marta shouted from behind me.

"Evinrude disappeared.

"'Rose Constantine,' said she and when our eyes met, she shook her index finger at me as if it were a pistol, pointed at the red motorbike in the centre of the courtyard, at me and then her temple, and announced in final warning, 'Tio Antonio.'

"I stumbled inside at dusk with a heavy heart, for it wasn't infatuation but love, violent and orange as Guiria's sunset; but sleep eluded me.

"I never heard any noises but the baker who rents the first room with his family woke me with his terrified shouting, 'Argenis! Argenis!'

"I stood on the bed and tiptoed to reach the high porthole that looked down at the courtyard. The baker's voice hollered to the half-crazy man who stumbled out of his room in a stupor. All Argenis managed to utter was, 'Uh! Uh! Uh!'

"Meanwhile, Señor Vasquez, that's the baker, shouted orders like any distinguished general to his junior ranking soldier, Argenis: 'Wake up the ladies! Put on the lights! Fetch a machete! Check the front door!'

"I was looking on from the darkness of my room, closest to the terrace, wet with fear. Argenis disappeared and returned to the courtyard armed with a dull cutlass, and wearing loose, white, awful underpants.

"'To the battlefield!' Señor Simón Vasquez shouted from behind the door for he was unprepared to die for Evinrude.

"'Dónde están?' Argenis quavered. 'Dónde están?'

"He seemed ready to fight, but unprepared to die. The other occupied apartments were black with fear for there were three, dreadful bandits, armed to the teeth, rummaging through cupboards, drawers and overturned pans. While I worried for Evinrude's life, a bandit was striking him unconscious, and another was beating the one-legged diabetic, whom Señor Vasquez had mentioned but I hadn't met, on his healthy leg. The third thief cornered Argenis outside the baker's room.

"'Fight!' Señor Vasquez urged without showing his face. 'Fight as if your life depends on it, Argenis! Man your station!'

"I screamed when another faceless bandit appeared in the dull courtyard and fired into the door and walls of the baker's abode. The thieves must have known the family was poor because they never worried with them.

"There was a final shout and the thud of fleeing feet on mud.

"Silence.

"Then, without any warning, Evinrude's motorcycle roared to life and out of the courtyard. More silence. Then darkness and all was still, as if the bandits' escapade were but a mocking nightmare.

"The police arrived at three in the morning, two hours after the ordeal and a moment before Evinrude regained consciousness. Some drunks had strayed into the courtyard; to interfere rather than help. Argenis was leaning against the doorway to his apartment, white with shock, his right hand holding up his oversized trousers, the dull machete hanging from his left. Señora Vasquez was standing in the courtyard, cradling the shaken Pedro. The baker was sleeping inside with Carmen and Jose who had never stirred during the imbroglio. The one-legged man, whose name I cannot recall, was sitting in a wheelchair outside his room waiting for an ambulance. Evinrude had been taken to my room and was being mothered by Aunty Marta. The two police officers interviewed him in machinegun Spanish and casualness that would shock any Trinidadian. The thieves had whispered away his laptop and every compact disc but it was the red motorcycle he cried for. The police left with perfunctory promises to be on high alert but my wits had been shattered and the safety daylight brings comforted everyone but me.

"At midday Aunty Marta and Evinrude walked me past the one-legged man, mind you he was still waiting on an ambulance, and to the port where I boarded the ferry bound for Trinidad, fear in my mind and love in my heart. He and I hugged under the watchful eyes of Aunty Marta but he still managed to slip me a note written in a familiar, crooked hand, the contents of which I need not discuss with you.

"Pardon me, officer, but I must be on my way! Are we through? Thank you. Yes, perhaps, I will send Evinrude messages in bottles made in Trinidad!"

Ariel

The first time I see Ariel I fall in love. She have shape for so, a bubbly face and wide hips, like a two litre swee' drink, but she waist narrow and she stomach chisel out, like them gyul and them in milk advertisement. She was a lil brown skin *chick* with hair that more curly than straight. She voluptuous too. I did already make up my mind that she nice too bad, so when I see how brown and crooked she teeth was I didn't study it. The first time I talk to Ariel was in Trincity Mall, where she was wo'king selling sweetie in a lil booth that sold popcorn too. I diabetic but I want to engage in conversation bad, so I buying like is first time.

"How old you is, Miss?"

She close she mouth and jerk back. "Why you want to know that?"

I love she more. "I find you nice," I say, popping a sweetie in my mouth. My sugar raise instantly. "I could get your phone number?"

"You don't find you moving kind of fast? You ain't even know my name."

I use the opening and ask she.

The way she say *Ariel*, she lips look thick and nice.

"Ariel," I say, liking its appeal. Smooth like honey: "That is a name for angels." The blush I get tell me things in my favour. Before I leave I had she phone number.

Two days later I gone to buy more sweetie. By this time is over sixty dollars I spend and I can't even eat the things. Me and Ariel talking cool, she giving me all the right signs: laughing at my jokes; twirling her hair while listening; smiling at my staler jokes; slapping my arms for the funnier ones. When a joke was *kixy*, she hid her lips and nose with five upright fingers, and her eyes twinkled as she giggled into her palm.

In time, the question of age come up. I get nervous because I guessing from all she *experience* she much older than me.

"Come on," she say, "tell me how much years you have." She leaned over the counter and tugged me closer with her forefinger.

"Answer me first nah," I pleaded, love in m' eyes. I watching she elbows and fingers and find they looking little pleated so I frighten to tell she the truth. So I lie and say I is nineteen. This time I is sixteen. My voice ain't even crack yet, but my lie work good; I a little big for my age.

"Oh that's not bad," she said, smiling, twirling her hair. "I is twenty-three." She lift a brow. She chewing down hard on a gum.

I confess, "I like you still." I want to say love, because it in my heart, but I know it a little too early.

Ariel smiled. The chick was gorgeous!

I walk home that night, thinking: hmm, she is really seven years older. I would not lie, although I was in love, I think I had my first taste of being a real man. I mean, imagine I hook up with someone as experienced as Ariel.

I start to beg my mother for extra money, and what I used to spend on games (back in them days is seventy-five cents for a coin), I saving. Two months later I buy a gift for my chick, a cheap ceramic surfboard with three words on its cherry-pink face.

Two weeks later, Ariel home in my mother house for my parents' anniversary. I making all kind of joke and confiding how she is the one, and I hoping that my big brother don't sell out my re'l age. My father only watching she over a tall plate o' roti. I could tell he trying to calculate something, because he had that look on he face.

I realise one thing that night: Ariel could eat. She bust up 'bout two, good plate o' roti and curry, and sit down rubbing she belly. Meanwhile, I doing the maths, thinking I need a work to maintain she. That night, a fellar name Robert picked Ariel up from the anniversary party, a cool red man, who mommy say could o' pass for we family, so she give him a plate o' food. When they leave, daddy corner me.

"Son, that girl, how old she is? She looks like a grown woman." When I tell him twenty-three, he shake he head. "Never happen! She older than that. You ain't see she elbows and toes?"

I tell the old man I in love and she could be older than that I ain't care because she is the woman I going to marry.

Time pass. Every day I in the mall checking Ariel, trying to get closer, trying to win her affection. I even stop buying sweetie. Instead I started taking her any cheap, meaningful gifts I could find. One day, I find she looking sad.

I say, "Babes, wha' happen? Talk to me *nah.*"

"I have something to confess," she say. "I is not twenty-three. I is twenty-eight."

"I still love you," I said, and it felt so good to say it that I smiled. We hug up and she give me a big kiss.

I wake up whole night, staring at the ceiling, counting all the knot in the wood until is morning. At ten o'clock when I walk in the mall, my chest stick out, like I wearing a bullet proof vest. Ariel *dolls up*.

"I could run away early," she told me. "Le' we go home by me. You have your car?"

I shame to tell the girl I too young to have my licence, so I tell she how daddy borrow my car. She get vex. We travel to Arima then take a taxi to Wallerfield, a community of small houses, fenced yards and high bush, just off the highway.

"You does go drags on Thursdays?" she ask, pointing in the direction of the abandoned airstrip.

"Only when I racing," I say, taking my time on the gravel road. I want to ask she whether or not she is a squatter, because Wallerfield have that look and feel. A car coming towards us stopped and Ariel introduced me to she mother, she mother man and she stepsister. They looked like squatters. A child sitting down on the mother lap. When they ask if we want to go beach, we blank them.

Five minutes inside Ariel's house, my bladder weak. I never encounter anything like this, where I home alone with a chick, much less my woman. When we gone in she bedroom, she show me a mattress on the ground.

I say, "Wha' happen you have a child or what?"

She laugh and say yes.

I smile, but I worried. I studying I have to mind child. I tell she I want to pee. She show me the bathroom and after I number one, I gone to wash my hand. While it not relevant to the story, the strangest thing happen: I don't know if the pipe was rusty or if it get tie-up with the cesspit, but a thick, nasty, brown paste shoot out. I spend fifteen minutes scrubbing my hand. I use perfumes that was on the sink. I use detergent on the ground next to the toilet. I use a green mouthwash I know Trincity Mall does sell in the ten dollars store. I rub and I rub.

When I gone back in the bedroom, Ariel lie down on the mattress naked as she born. Her lips folded. She squeezing her breasts, like she testing ripe papaws for firmness. My bladder full up again.

"Come," she said.

I smell my hands. "I want to go home." I started to cry. Then I ran away.

One week later, I went to the mall. I buy some sweetie, but Ariel blue vex, only making a little eye contact, gauging me as if I planning to shoplift. I buy some more sweetie but she still not talking.

"Girl, look here," I say, "I want to talk to you tonight, okay. Where I living it have a spot under a tree. It re'l nice. No frog or mosquito, only a lil sand fly." I coax and I coax.

That night we gone by the spot. I playing man because my brother tell me what to do. I stroking she hair, brushing she lips with mine, massaging her feet. But I not getting any reaction. When I get fed up, I hold she hand and walk home. We sit down on a concrete step outside my neighbour house, another "love nest" with a hibiscus hedge as a backdrop. A few minutes into the silence, the same fellar who pick she up from my parents' anniversary, as if by magic, strolled past.

He stopped.

They spoke.

I tried to listen, my heart still in pieces.

Ariel stood before me, like she is Wonder Woman. "This is Robert."

I watch him *cut eye*. He was a big red man. "And?"

"Well," she say, "we have been seeing each other for the past six months."

I do the maths. I know Ariel about that long.

"I'm sorry," Ariel said, "but I never loved you."

Ariel and Robert left.

I cried. I cried like a sixteen-year-old. I folded my hands across my knees and rested my head on top, blinded by grief. My tears fell on the rough reality below. I knew my heart would ache for an eternity. Someone sat next to me. It was dad. He knew what was wrong. But his words sounded like a lecture. I was in love. I didn't care for proverbs like 'a pretty face without personality is dead.' I counted his boy days as nothing. I cried for two weeks, waking every morning only to remember that my heart was broken.

Then, I decide is time to confront Ariel. I spied her from a distance. She was talking to a boy I knew, smiling, twirling her hair, brown smiles plastered across her face. I reasoned. I saw a happy-go-lucky girl. I wondered if she had even thought of me while I spent forever shedding tears. She showed nothing that could prove it. Why should I be unhappy, when she wasn't? Why should I die while she lived?

I had five dollars in my pocket. I looked at her one last time and headed for the arcade.

Simon's rant

We all talk about crime and truly hate it with a passion. Don't you? Of course you do! Murders, rapes, kidnappings, you name it we have it, and in great quantities too. Newspaper journalists and TV reporters need not worry, because right around the corner is another horror story. Gangs rivaling with each other, shooting up basketball courts, spraying bullets like mad. Innocent or not so innocent bystanders catching one or two of the unnecessary marked for death bullets.

Young woman, walking through a lonely track, after a hard day's work of frying chicken, diverted to an abandoned house. Brutal rape follows for just a couple seconds and as easy as that, an old, dirty piece of rope wrapped around her neck and the rapist decides that she dies. Crystal, the six year old, waits to see mummy coming through the front gate, anxious for a piece of chicken. Next time she sees her, is in a cheap, light blue casket.

Yes. You like how things going in this country? Tell me, you like it?

Love triangle gone sour, the mark buss and man gone crazy. Four dead: wife, *horner man* and child. Dass can't take jail so he dead too. You like this place?

You reach home, or you wonder if you really did because the whole place turned over. Fridge wide open, kitchen drawers out, place in a total frenzy like if a tornado pass through. You happy?

"Is the government! No! Is the police! Is the cocaine! Is the weed! Nah, is the society!"

But tell me: what about your family?

Chasing sevens

Kenrick Maraj lived with his parents in the last mud house on Temple Street and although they had a zinc roof overhead and ate well their disposition embarrassed him. Then there was the donkey cart which his father eventually sold and replaced with an old white van; never mind the van bucked and belched and moved slower than the donkey walked. Then, as if to mock Kenrick's pride, a multimillion-dollar construction company cleared the sugarcane fields surrounding Dinsley Village and began erecting concrete flats and *upstairs* houses that made him sour with envy. Around that time his parents lost their jobs as cane cutters with the sugar factory. His mother became a potter, his father a manure salesman, and on weekends while other children were at home watching Saturday morning cartoons, Kenrick and his father journeyed to *Gerard Stables* in the old white van.

It was a chilly Saturday morning. Kenrick lay face down in the tray. Bucking, the van slowed and stopped at a traffic light. He peeked over the rail but when a girl in the Mercedes behind pointed and laughed, he ducked. The light blinked green, the van swung off the highway, sped south along a road laden with potholes and turned right at a forked junction. Here the stink of uncured manure burnt his nostrils. Keeping low, he eased himself up and looked around: a chainlink fence, with barbed wire on top, ran parallel to the road and stretched back to the highway, enclosing the Santa Rosa racetrack. Opposite, stables lined the road. He sat up, cupped his face with both hands and peered through the van's rear glass, temporarily amused that it fogged whenever he exhaled. Good, no sign of anyone except, way beyond the racetrack's stadium, a man riding a tricycle fitted with a beach umbrella. Bucking still, the van entered *Gerard Stables*, lurched and parked below a ficus tree. The van coughed and died in a cloud of white smoke.

When his father exited the van Kenrick hopped out of the tray reluctantly. Underfoot the dirt was soggy and caked with yellow leaves. He walked on tiptoe across the yard to an endless lane of concrete stalls that stretched in either direction. Horses peeked out. Flies buzzed around. Three old-timers, sitting on crocus bags with their backs to a stall used as the tool shed, were sharing a cigarette. Immediately around them were white bags half-filled with manure, their necks rolled down. Kenrick's father, gesturing to a mound of horse manure beside the van, spoke to the Indian man in the middle.

Meanwhile, Kenrick wandered along the stalls, reaching out to horses and quickly pulling his hand away. In passing, he slapped two or three of them and giggled crazily. When he came to a narrow passageway between two empty stables, he glanced back. His father had lowered the van's rails and was shovelling manure into the tray. Kenrick ducked inside the passage and followed it to the backyard, where a horse was walking in circles inside an automated exerciser, a big, circular tank with a metal wall the length of its diameter. As the wall rotated, urging the horse forward, the exerciser shuddered, creaked and groaned, like his father's van. Smiling thinly, he stared until his amusement dwindled.

Five stalls away, an enormously fat, ruddy groomsman, barebacked and bald-headed, stood wiping his hands with a dirty towel and speaking to a jockey on horseback – when the jockey noticed Kenrick, he glared and passed a syringe to the groomsman who, fumbling, tucked it into his back pocket. Kenrick gasped, for the horse, snorting and outfitted in gold, appeared terrifying and handsome; and the jockey – well, donned in gold silks, goggles, riding boots and an unbuckled helmet – looked mighty fine. He sat on the horse with his legs tucked in, high up, and balanced a whip across his knees. The groomsman cursed and signalled "be right back" to the jockey when Kenrick's father shouted from out front.

"Nice horsey," Kenrick said. He had approached the jockey on horseback.

The jockey, no bigger than a sixteen-year-old boy, was Indian. He spoke like an Englishman. "*Beautiful* son-of-a-gun, huh?" He winked and stroked his mount like a good dog. "A thorough-bred, you know."

"Could run fast?"

"Like the devil."

"Wha's she name?"

The jockey scoffed and stared contemptuously. "It's a *he*… *Heptad*."

"Wha' *Heptad* mean?"

Smirking, the jockey snatched up his whip and, stabbing his chest, said, "That's for me to know," and pointing down at Kenrick, "and you to find out."

"I could touch her?"

"Are you an ass, boy? Do you think *your* father could afford this horse? Get away from me!"

Kenrick ran crying to his father as if the jockey had whipped him. Annoyed, the father dipped in his pocket, extracted a ball of trash, and sifted through coins, paper and matchsticks. He grunted then hollered at a *Snowcone Man* riding past the stable on a tricycle equipped with a beach umbrella, icebox and dispensers containing colourful syrups that attracted flies. He dismounted, removed a rag from his back pocket and flicked it over his shoulder. He removed a Styrofoam cup from a plastic bag tied to the umbrella. Smiling, he encouraged his young customer closer. When he opened the icebox, cold air rushed over Kenrick's neck and face. *The Snowcone Man* packed the cup with crushed ice. Red and yellow syrup went on top. He stuck the *snowcone* through with a straw, wiped the brim with his rag and passed the *snowcone* to Kenrick who picked a hole, sucked up chunks of coloured ice and sighed, "Mmm!" It was *good* yet incomplete, like a *doubles* without pepper.

"Pa," Kenrick begged, "I could ge' condense' milk on top?"

"Boy, tha's *big shot* thing! Say thank goodness you even ge' a *snowcone*." He counted twenty three cents and paid the *Snowcone Man*. "Ge' in the van, and go fast!"

But the *Snowcone Man* stopped Kenrick and, slowly, drained condensed milk on top his *snowcone* at no additional cost. "Try it, y'u go like it."

"I like it," Kenrick said and ran off and joined the horse manure in the tray.

As the van headed for the highway, he vowed: I will own a *racing horse* one day. Smiling at the big shot idea, he gobbled his *snowcone* and flung the Styrofoam cup on the road. When the van chugged into Dinsley, his fantasies ebbed and he lay flat in the dung, but villagers walking along the road saw him and shouted in shrill mockery, *"Manure on the outside!"*

Finally the van turned into Temple Street, bucked along a stretch lined with mud houses, unfenced yards and *jhandis* and stalled in front the last house. The yard was crowded with rows of clay pots, balusters and deyas which snaked below the shed joined to the house; on the opposite side there was an outdoor bathroom built with four sheets of upright zinc; in the backyard, a home oven for baking clay inventions. West of the house was a savannah surrounded by samaan trees and infested with cricketers. Kites fluttered over an orange-roofed pavilion.

"I want to play cricket," Kenrick sulked. He was sitting on top the van's hood.

"You want to wo'k," his father snapped as he untied the ropes holding the rails together. The rails fell with a bang. "Go fas' an' ge' the shovel and crocus bags."

Beneath the shed, among clay images as tall as children, Kenrick's mother was on all fours, hunched over a trough. She was kneading cow dung and clay with her bare hands.

"The *chulha* need *lepaying*," she said without looking up. "I want you *dab* it, but finish with y'u' pa first."

Kenrick rolled his eyes and mouthed a cuss word. "Ma, I wan' to make a kite."

"Boy, listen!" His mother stopped her work and glared. She pointed, dung and clay between her fingers like peanut butter webs. "Boy, y'u have wo'k to do, y'u better thank God y'u not living India."

"I want a horse for Christmas."

"Boy! Wha' *stupidness* you talking? Go fas' an' ge' the shovel and crocus bags before I break your ass."

Where the shed met the backyard there was a blue drum stuffed with tools. The shovel was resting against the back wall with the crocus bags stuffed through its handle like rolled up newspapers. That day, as he shovelled horse dung into bags and drove around upper-class neighbourhoods sitting in the tray, squeaking a horn and shrieking, "*Manure on the outside*," he dreamed of owning a horse.

One day… one day.

Kenrick's discontentment curdled during his teenage years for his parents worked nonstop, fussed a lot and horded their earnings. None of their money went towards repairing the van or building a brick house. To escape them he quit work, choosing instead to spend his time in the Dinsley Savannah.

On his fourteenth birthday he made a kite with a copybook page, *cocoyea* (dried coconut frond) bent like a bow and wrapped closely with red thread, a bed sheet tail and vicious-smelling glue. On his way to the savannah he met Baljan sitting under a samaan tree with exposed roots like arthritic fingers, smoking a joint and drinking a Guinness. Baljan, handsome and Indian, was from a rich family. He was sixteen. Chuckling, he pointed at Kenrick's kite and asked:

"You ever sniff glue?"

Over the years Baljan introduced Kenrick to every vice imaginable. He didn't care for smoking, drinking or too much girls but when Baljan took him to a racing pool, *oh boy, talk about excitement.* The thrill began opposite *Goldwood Racing Pool,* a building like a three-storey cardboard box cut with saloon doors. Above the entrance was an intricate wood carving of horses with fiery manes galloping towards a pot of gold in the centre. Without looking left and right he ran across the main road, keeping ahead of Baljan, and as planned he didn't linger but inhaled and slipped past the saloon doors like a cocksure cowboy.

Inside, crumpled paper, cigarette butts and beer caps littered the floor. Among the zombie gamblers, Kenrick didn't recognise anyone. Relieved, he exhaled and the gambler's haven came alive: the breathless commentaries over suspended speakers, the gamblers hanging on to every word and scratching racing forms like executives signing million dollar cheques. Most patrons, mainly old men, wore netted caps and Amazonian shirts tucked inside three-quarter denim pants. Above the teller's den, clocks kept time for Trinidad, Tampa, Yorkshire and Ireland. Outside the booth, a mixed woman, wearing high heeled shoes and a grey business suit with accessories, sat with her legs crossed. She had a pencil behind her ear and her right shoe hung loosely from her toes. She stood and greeted Baljan with a hug. When he introduced her to Kenrick as The Guru, she smiled as if in possession of many secrets.

"You 's a guru?" Kenrick scoffed. He had assumed all gurus were old Indian men with great white beards and slack jockey shorts.

"I am *The Horse Guru,*" she replied, her eyes proud and fierce. "You don't know about me? Every serious gambler knows me." She opened a wallet she had removed from her purse. "Here's my card."

Accepting, he lifted his brows, pushed out his bottom lip and uttered a shrill, "Humph!" He read the card aloud, "The Horse Guru, Sports Journalist," flipped it over and frowned.

"Something's bothering you," she said. "What is it?"

"Why you' parents name y'u The Horse Guru?"

Puzzled, she glanced at Baljan then burst into a bout of quiet, uncontrollable laughter. Sniffing, she wiped her eyes. "The Horse Guru is my penname."

"Wha' qualifications you have?" Kenrick challenged.

"Be nice," Baljan said and chuckled nervously.

"I will, and I can speak for myself," The Horse Guru said, silencing them with her eyes and palms. "I interview local owners and trainers and visit practice sessions." She passed a racing form captioned *Tampa Bay Racing*. "In horse racing it isn't only about the highest odds. Take a look at *Running-WithGas*. *Angel Eyes* is also in the two o'clock race. The former has better results on the furlongs but she's fresh out of surgery and her trainer, Bob Colt, is going through a divorce. *Angel Eyes* is the one to watch. She gives trouble in the gates true, but her performance on the tracks particularly firm ground has steadily improved over a six-month period; Kathleen Wilson, her trainer and a feminist, is also excellent." It took her another minute to explain why the other horses would never, not in a million years, place or show.

Lips pursed, Kenrick lifted his eyebrows and perused the form, putting columns into perspective. He found the lowest odds, traced his finger to the corresponding horse and passed the form to The Horse Guru.

"What 'bout *Duck and Run*?" he asked.

Without checking the racing form, she blurted, "Tut-tut! 30 to 1? Please oh please! *RunningWithGas* and *Angel Eyes*, those are the *in the money* horses." Baljan excused himself and went to the teller.

Kenrick's hands disappeared inside his pants pockets. He stared at his shoes then at the four hanging clocks. "I's almos' two o'clock, y'u wan' to bet on it?"

"Nice try," The Horse Guru smirked, "but I don't gamble."

"I will defy the odds and bet *Duck and Run*."

"Suit yourself, *boy*."

Muttering, he went to counter, feeling an icy void in his stomach as he pushed between Baljan and the teller. "Do you mind?" he said and Baljan clumsily scooped up his receipts, moved away and sat. Behind the counter, Bertrand Brown, red-skinned and stern, sat on a stool with his legs propped up and opened in a kind of monkey-stance. He resembled a malnourished pitbull.

"Wha's the smallest bet?" Kenrick asked.

Bertrand Brown nodded at a sign taped to the counter. Kenrick counted fifty cents but he reasoned a bigger bet more profitable so he wagered three dollars, all his money, on *Duck and Run*. He collected his receipt and turned just as The Horse Guru slipped out the racing pool. Kenrick sat beside Baljan and stared at the saloon doors until they stopped swinging.

"Who was tha' woman?" he asked.

"An expert on horses," Baljan said and chuckled. "She writes weekly columns, sharing tips."

"She mus' be can't write because she can't even talk prop'ly."

"She usually has pretty good tips," Baljan shrugged. "I won a couple forecasts and aggregates from reading her articles."

Kenrick shrugged indifferently. "Who you bet on?"

"I have a win on *Angel Eyes*, and a win and place on *RunningWithGas*."

"No good," Kenrick said. "High odds but low payouts."

"Who's your favourite?"

"Tha's personal," Kenrick scowled.

At two o'clock Trinidad time the racing pool went up on its toes when a commentator rattled over *Goldwood's* speaker system but Kenrick felt alone. One hand propped up his face, the other went across his knees; and staring at the floor he pumped his feet and urged *Duck and Run*. It unnerved him that Baljan scratched his head and yawned. Eyes closed, Kenrick leaned back and played his chest like a drum, head tilted towards the noise as if to a narcotic that would lift his spirits. Now, listening to the commentator, he pictured *Angel Eyes* two lengths ahead of *RunningWithGas*, with *Duck and Run* struggling behind — and suddenly the race resolved. Kenrick cursed and Baljan collected on *Angel Eyes* and *RunningWithGas*.

The racing pool more than anything fuelled Kenrick's ambition to own a horse. Many Septembers later, when he had grown older, Mounted Branch hired his father to "dispose" of an injured horse which he intervened and saved. His dream of owning a horse was a reality. This realisation bolstered his ego. Kenrick became *the man*.

Next morning Kenrick borrowed a khaki suit and red tie from Baljan and towards evening led *GoFast* to Dinsley junction. It brought him great pleasure that people stopped and stared and pointed. Cars screeched and swerved. A car even crashed into the traffic lights in front the pharmacy. People waved and whistled. Chinese men and women wearing paper hats and holding knives peeked past restaurant doors and gazed between *GoFast* and each other, talking excitedly among themselves; when Kenrick noticed them he feared for *GoFast's* safety and hurried along.

Overwhelmed by this fanfare, Kenrick ignored *GoFast's* limp and continued along the main road gathering followers until he arrived at *Goldwood Racing Pool*, reopened only the day before after two years of renovations. Folks who didn't care for Kenrick rushed outside and congratulated him. They wanted to know everything about *GoFast*. "When it racing?" a man asked. When another man stroked *GoFast*, Kenrick grabbed his hand and barked, "Doh do tha', doh do tha'! You want to *maljoe* m' horse?" When the crowd thinned, Kenrick tied *GoFast* to a van, held his breath and shoved open tinted double doors to the racing pool.

Inside *Goldwood Racing Pool* hanging televisions had replaced the speaker system. There were slot machines. Tellers behind protective glass took bets. Management had replaced itchy wooden chairs with padded plastic versions. The only relics were the zombie gamblers, that rumshop smell, paper scraps littering the floor; and The Horse Guru, sitting further back in her usual spot, tapping her teeth with a pencil, busy eyes locked on the screens. Kenrick neatened his hair and approached her.

"I want you write an article 'bout me," he said.

"*Good afternoon*, Kenrick." The Horse Guru jotted in her notebook. "Can I help you?"

"I have a winning horse outside."

"I heard the commotion," she said and stood. She grabbed up her purse, slung it over her shoulder and folded her arms. "Does your *green horse* warrant an article? Excuse me Kenrick, and good day."

Kenrick scowled, wiped his face with the back of his forearm and sat. The chair was uncomfortably warm. He shifted until The Horse Guru's fire left his seat. The overhead televisions advised another race in six minutes. Kenrick scanned the line up for the horse with the lowest odds – *Why Not Me?* – then went to the ticket counter. Two or three minutes before the race, The Horse Guru stormed inside and, to everyone's amusement, collared Kenrick and dragged him outside.

"What nonsense is this?" she said, pointing at *GoFast*. "This poor creature is almost lame with a splint and you're *parading* her?"

Kenrick jerked away and dusted Baljan's suit. "Bu' wha' the ass wrong with you, woman? Just-so-just-so you go hold on to *my* suit and rough me up?"

The Horse Guru's squint deepened. "You're such an idiot."

A crowd had gathered. *Goldwood* patrons who had congratulated Kenrick earlier, rebuked him. They argued that a splint was as troublesome as a broken leg. They wondered aloud whether *GoFast* should be shot. Kenrick shoved a man who startled *GoFast*. Meanwhile, The Horse Guru hailed a passing van and for a small fee negotiated a ride for *GoFast* back to Dinsley.

With *GoFast* secured and The Horse Guru riding up front, the van crawled along the main road, the driver hunched over and worried by the "ass" accompanying the horse; he consulted his rearview mirror without pause. Standing beside

GoFast, Kenrick, jacket unbuttoned and red tie blowing smartly over his shoulder, waved to pedestrians and drivers until his arms hurt. When the driver doubled-checked his mirrors, indicated and turned into Dinsley Village, the sky was turquoise, the sunset crimson. Four blocks down, he signalled, navigated into Temple Street and drove to Kenrick's parents' mud house at the end. "You'll be seeing me tomorrow," The Horse Guru said when Kenrick and *GoFast* disembarked then the van took her away.

Next morning as his parents urged him from bed, Kenrick stretched and moaned and twisted in the sheets for the mud house was dim and cool. Eventually, they wearied him. He rubbed his eyes and peered through the louvers. A grey sky hung low and mist sat still in crevices along the bumpy northern range. Outside, *GoFast* whinnied. Fanning herself and breathless, Kenrick's mother passed him a jersey and trousers.

"Gosh Kenrick," she squeaked, "it have a nice gyul outside who come to see y'u. She skin re'l *nice* and *clear.*"

"And tall too," his father said. "You *cyar* keep a nice woman like tha' waiting."

Annoyed, Kenrick dressed. His father doused him with cologne and they led him into the dining room, one proud parent on either side. The Horse Guru sat at a small table cramped in one corner and draped with plastic, a bell and hibiscus arrangement in a glass of water on top. Furniture covered with blankets separated this eating area from the living room. Under the front window was an old-fashioned box television covered with a doily. Muttering, Kenrick flushed. His father smiled and his mother pulled a chair for him.

"Anything to eat or drink Miss Barbara?" Kenrick's parents asked together, smiling warmly.

"Another glass of water will be fine thanks."

When his parents stepped outside, The Horse Guru extolled them but Kenrick grunted. The Horse Guru leaned forward and rested her palms face up on the table.

"You know," she said and interlocked her fingers, "I live in Caura Valley. When I was six I saw a horse for the first time. *Belflair* was her name."

"*Belflair*? That name sounds familiar. Who owned her?"

"Mr. Bertrand Brown, my uncle."

"I know Bertrand," Kenrick said, roving eyes searching his memory.

"Yes, you'd know him. Before they renovated the racing pool he collected bets, a small, red-skinned man, bald-headed, never smiled much."

Nodding, Kenrick said, "Tha' was m' boy! He tell me about *Belflair* a'ready, bu' I always say he talking crap."

"Really? Yes, *Belflair* was real and he pushed her from Sunday to Sunday, over-trained her actually. I could still hear *Belflair* galloping along the pitch road in front our house. And on their way back it thrilled me to hear the clickety-click of her shoes. I'd rush outside to see them." The Horse Guru smiled and shook her head. "Eventually my uncle got *Belflair* into a race."

"They win?" Kenrick asked.

"*Belflair* showed but never raced again. A vet had to put her to sleep."

Kenrick's mother entered balancing three plates, a cup of tea and a glass pitcher with water and ice cubes. Expressing that she really wasn't hungry, The Horse Guru stood and transferred the hibiscus arrangement to a chest of drawers behind her.

"Please sit Miss Barbara!" Kenrick's mother insisted, setting the pitcher down. "It haves no need for you to get up. No need at all. You just eat as much as you want and don't worry there's plenty."

The cup of tea and a plate heaped with mashed potatoes went before Kenrick. "Ma, you know I don't like pimento," Kenrick said but ignoring him, his mother set down a plate heaped with light-brown fried potatoes before the guest. The third plate contained *sada* roti wrapped in cloth. This went between Kenrick and The Horse Guru.

"If you want more, Miss Barbara, just let me know," Kenrick's mother said.

"Your *aloo* looks and smells fantastic," The Horse Guru said. "It drives me insane that I never can get it this creamy brown."

"You mean the *bun bun*?" Kenrick said. "Tha's my favourite part."

"It so funny to hear somebody like you say *aloo*," Kenrick's mother said. She smiled mischievously at her son and left the room.

"Le' we talk business," Kenrick said. "You think it go be easy to ge' *GoFast* in a race?" Keeping his eyes on The Horse Guru he reached to the plate between them, unfolded the cloth and took two slices of roti, cut like pizza and dusted with flour.

"Your priority is healing *GoFast*," The Horse Guru replied. "She's an old police horse."

"She had a sweet wo'k," Kenrick joked.

"Stay focussed," The Horse Guru said. "She spent her days walking on hard surfaces."

Kenrick nodded complacently. When they finished eating his mother cleared the table. The Horse Guru retrieved her shoes from a mat by the door and she and Kenrick went outside. The cold hadn't yet left the earth and mist still hung between the samaan trees lining the savannah. The Horse Guru crossed her arms but stopped rubbing them and frowned at *GoFast's* stall, a knee-high enclosure built of overlapping galvanise and joined to the house's back wall. She turned to Kenrick and tilted her head.

"Kenrick, do you own a saddle or bridle?" She smiled thinly when Kenrick shook his head. "Rehabilitate *GoFast* and I'll loan you both." Before leaving, she tipped him on horse care and gave him laminated leaflets on the subject.

During the first month of *GoFast's* rehabilitation, The Horse Guru visited Dinsley Village on Wednesdays but even with her help Kenrick hated the tedious work. However, motivated by the prospect of a saddle and bridle, he woke at dawn every day, armed himself with a sickle and walked south across the savannah to a vacant lot patched with high bush. He chopped without discrimination, reasoning *GoFast* could pick and choose what she liked. By the second week responsibility wearied Kenrick but he mucked out the stall and at lunchtime The Horse Guru arrived by taxi. The driver offloaded a crocus bag then left. Kenrick sat in the hammock parallel to the backyard.

"Wha's tha'?" he asked, pointing.

"Horse pellets," grunted The Horse Guru in passing. She hiked up her skirt, entered *GoFast's* stall and whispering intimately, stooped and inspected the animal's left leg. Still stooping, she glanced at Kenrick and smiled thinly. "Are you icing her leg every day?"

Kenrick rose and settled her concern with his best smile.

"I am very pleased. Now, those pellets, you must store them in a dry place and don't overfeed her! She mustn't be too heavy. Are you taking her out to graze on afternoons?"

"Yes, yes," Kenrick said and capsized the plastic barrel with his father's tools, causing such a ruckus his mother, inside her bedroom, complained. Kenrick rolled his eyes. "You see what I does have to deal with?" After they shoved the pellets inside, Kenrick helped the barrel into an upright position and kicked his father's tools under the table with the earthen *chulha* stove on top. He and The Horse Guru stood intimately close.

"Kenrick," she said and he stared at her. "Are you taking care of *GoFast* or simply telling me what I want to hear?"

Kenrick bit his lip and nodded. He smiled when The Horse Guru said she'd soon bring him the saddle and bridle. The following Wednesday she delivered on her promise and warned Kenrick not to push *GoFast* too hard, at least not for two months, by which time, with treatment, the splint should go *cold*. But that night, inspecting the saddle and bridle in his bedroom, Kenrick reckoned he should find himself a jockey. Next day he went around Dinsley Village advertising the post.

Two days after Kenrick got the saddle and bridle, he invited applicants to the Dinsley Savannah. Despite the sun a line stretched around the perimeter. From the sidelines a small crowd observed the interviews. Pointing, they sneered at the potentials and doubled over laughing when the horse owner disparaged them. *This one*, no way, way too tall; *that one*, *jeez-an-ages*, fat and clumsy, he might break *GoFast's* legs; Baljan had a good size, but he was a big drinker; and *the other*, damn good you know but a girl! Finally John Boy, a lad of seventeen, earned the job because standing at five-feet-three-inches, thin and angular, with a head shaped like a red bean, Kenrick thought he suited the role.

On day one, John Boy slipped, fell and catapulted off *Go-Fast*. Kenrick cursed. Kenrick screamed. Kenrick told John Boy what he thought of his mother. Kenrick kicked heaps of dried grass. The trio became a spectacle. Instead of *"Manure on the outside!"* folks called Kenrick obscene names.

In late October, around the same time Kenrick's parents left him in charge of the family's manure business and went on a tour across India, other problems surfaced. *Damn animal could really eat*, he thought as *GoFast* munched down the last bucket of pellets. *At least I have a saddle, a bridle and a savannah.*

During training one day The Horse Guru paid a surprise visit. She came upon Kenrick sitting below a samaan tree and John Boy peppering *GoFast* along the *paved* path that circled the savannah. Kenrick felt her purse smash against his head. The Horse Guru's cheeks went red and she gesticulated like a bible-crazed evangelist, her lips forming curse words without sound. Her anger and searing words were insurmountable and neither Kenrick nor John Boy resisted when, in passing, she jumped and dragged John Boy from *GoFast*, struck him twice in his head with her purse and stripped her uncle's saddle and bridle from *GoFast*.

"You go ge' a cattle boil in y'u' eye!" Kenrick shouted as The Horse Guru stormed away but he hid behind John Boy and shouted, "Hol' me back John Boy! Hol' me back!" when she turned and shook her fist.

Kenrick didn't plan to let The Horse Guru's concern for *GoFast's* splint stop training. Next day he and his team went to the savannah and John Boy spread a blanket on *GoFast's* back; she didn't fuss. But she rejected the lasso Kenrick proposed as a bridle. The following week, training involved John Boy running laps leading *GoFast* with Kenrick sitting in the pavilion, shielding his eyes from the stadium lights, mining his ears with a matchstick, talking to strangers, introducing himself as a famous horse owner and egging his horse and his jockey on each time they fumbled past.

"Y'u' riding gear is the problem," Kenrick said one evening. They had just come in from training. John Boy didn't respond; his shoulders were sore and his groin burned. He hobbled *GoFast* to her stall. In place of a saddle she wore a white cotton blanket bound by a piece of rope.

"John Boy, go and pu' on the damn light fo' the shed."

John Boy was stooping beneath *GoFast*. He untied and removed the cotton saddle, stood, folded and tossed it over his shoulder. "Remember the bulb blow last night, boss."

"*GoFast* should o' pee on y'u." Mumbling, Kenrick flicked open a hammock, lay back and propelled himself by pushing at the dirt floor with his hands. "Y'u' riding gear is the problem," he said again. "Wha' you think, John Boy?"

John Boy was grooming *GoFast* with a scrubbing brush. "She does whine a lot, boss, because she don't like her lasso bridle. Plus this blanket I using as a saddle kind o' uncomfortable."

"You mean *bladdle*!" Kenrick laughed and said it made John Boy walk like a *jamette*.

John Boy muttered.

Kenrick sat up and shouted, "Wha's tha' you say?"

"Nothing, boss."

"I need a saddle," Kenrick said and lay down again.

"Them thing not cheap, boss."

"You don't worry, I could *fix* that."

Caressing *GoFast's* face, John Boy walked around her so that her body hid Kenrick. He stopped grooming *GoFast* and gazed skyward. "Why not go see the guru, boss?"

"Who? The Horse Guru? You mad? I might crack she a slap."

"But she might have ideas."

"Why you don't go?" Kenrick stood and approached John Boy. "Do it for *GoFast*."

Next morning Kenrick settled in a hammock with nine or ten scratch cards in his lap and waited for John Boy who had walked three miles to The Horse Guru's Caura home. He returned at lunchtime soaked with sweat and toting an old saddle.

"Wha' she had to say 'bout me?" Kenrick asked, showing no interest in the saddle.

"Tell you as she say it?" John Boy said but his features tightened into sobriety when Kenrick glared. "Nothing, *she* only ask about *GoFast*, and apologise for hitting *me* with her purse."

"Nothing at all 'bout me?"

"*Nothing* really."

"How y'u mean nothing really?"

John Boy said, "She talked about some leaflets she gave you which," and now, speaking like a woman who imagined herself an aristocrat, "detail the fine art of bridle making."

Kenrick laughed at John Boy's impersonation of The Horse Guru, and while he fetched the leaflets from inside, John Boy located the bridle, went to the stall and slid back a sheet of galvanise creating a space large enough for *GoFast*. She took to the saddle but still didn't fancy the rope bridle.

Back in the hammock, armed with the leaflets, Kenrick explained the fine art of bridle making while John Boy settled *GoFast* and secured her stall.

"It soun' easy enough," John Boy said. "I have two old belt home."

"Ask around Dinsley too."

"Yes *boss*. I will need a measuring tape and buckles."

"What about the change I give you two days ago?" Kenrick asked. "Use that!"

John Boy took a leaflet from Kenrick and frowned. "I give my mother half, plus I want to use the change to buy saline. It say here that tha' good for open wounds and abras'ons."

Kenrick snapped, "Wha'ever; how *you* want to make the damn bridle *you* make it; right!"

It took John Boy two weeks to construct the bridle. He spent his days reading The Horse Guru's notes, measuring and re-measuring *GoFast's* face and dismantling old belts for their straps and buckles. A welder provided him with a bit held together with a solid ring on either side. A leather strap punched through with holes and held in place with shoelaces went around each ring. Next, he constructed the throatlatch and using two more rings weaved it to the straps holding the bit together. *GoFast* accepted the bridle and John Boy was proud of it. He no longer had to run ahead of *GoFast*. For weeks he rode her hard until she melted to skin and bones.

Because of financial constraints Kenrick had also lost weight. It irked his pride but he offered one minute rides at five dollars for kids, ten for adults. For one dollar a child could touch *GoFast*. Whatever money Kenrick made he hid away. On weekends John Boy bagged and sold manure with sawdust but Kenrick pocketed his earnings and on Sundays after John Boy had mucked out *GoFast's* stall and left for the night Kenrick rubbed gambler's oil behind his ears then went to the middle slot machine in Baljan's father's rumshop. He always bet big. Sometimes he carried a magnet in his pocket because he believed this "confused" the slot machines but the reels never landed on red sevens, although, they always came close.

Weeks passed. No one knew how but Kenrick fixed an entry for *GoFast* at the Santa Rosa racetrack. One month before the Boxing Day event he jogged to Baljan's father's rumshop. Outside, masons were paving the car park. Inside, a hanging television trapped in a cage showed a live T20 cricket match, West Indies versus Australia, one ball remaining, *Tiger* at the wicket, West Indies needing a massive six to win. The regulars, huddled around tables cluttered with bottles, grunted at Kenrick. Onscreen a blond bowler with bouncy hair bounded down the pitch; Kenrick swaggered to the table in front the television and climbed on top. His head bumped the cage, switching the television off. Someone flung a bottle that nicked Kenrick's forehead and a fight promptly broke out between two drunks who had wagered against each other. Nevertheless he published the news.

"Prove it!" someone shouted.

"Y'u jackass!" Kenrick drawled, skipping from table to table, meanwhile reaching into his pocket for a paper folded many times over. "Look my licence for owner and trainer *signed* by the racing authority! You feeling like a jackass now?"

Despite his previous blunder the patrons greeted Kenrick's news with rousing fanfare for as Baljan's father put it this race meant big things for Dinsley Village. A regular credited a beer for everyone including the masons out front. After, Baljan's father handed out another round. Others ran off to spread the news. Somewhere in the excitement a drunk trampled over fresh concrete and a black mason with broad shoulders cursed him bitterly. Shaking his head and thinking that black people re'lly liked attention, Kenrick noticed Baljan sitting on a stool in front a slot machine. He went to him. The slot machine had over three hundred credits. Placed on top were a beer, loose cigarettes, a Zippo and a magnet. Kenrick lit a cigarette and took two sharp pulls but didn't inhale.

"Baljan, y'u hear the news?" he asked and blew a cloud at the ceiling.

"Congrats," Baljan replied and Kenrick's smile widened. "I's the first time in my life I see my father share out drinks; you should buy another horse." Kenrick held his stomach and laughed so raucously that Baljan only stopped frowning when he stopped laughing. "What colours John Boy riding in?" he asked but Kenrick hadn't heard; the spinning reels and digital arpeggios thrilled him. The music stopped with the reels; Kenrick cursed.

"You betting too small." He leaned over Baljan, tapped *Max Credits* then *Bet*. The slot machine played happy music while the reels spun. "Ah; shit man! We miss the red sevens again."

"I *was* winning up to a moment ago," Baljan said sourly.

"We will get it don't worry." Kenrick bet sixteen credits again, cranked the lever and the reels spun happily – he thumped *Bet* and the reels stopped abruptly. "Shit boy Baljan, like you blight. We will get the sevens, I feeling it."

Kenrick gambled until Baljan's credits finished. Baljan was broke.

"Humph!" Kenrick stubbed out his cigarette on top the slot machine and said, "What colours he riding in? Well *Go-Fast* is a kind o' dark brown."

Baljan snapped, "Then John Boy should ride in a red bra and panty."

Kenrick stiffened and scoffed, "How I go do tha'? I cyar do that." (Baljan gazed at the slot machine as it went through its automated, winning cycle.) "John Boy finished the bridle, but waste of time!" Kenrick continued. "Me and *GoFast* have to look official fo' this race." (Baljan wiped his face downward.) "You even listening to me, Baljan?"

"Listening?" Baljan chuckled.

Wagging his forefinger, Kenrick said, almost as if cautioning Baljan, "I know wha' happen, you *wish* you was me, y'u jealous me." He punched Baljan's shoulder playfully. "On another note, y'u mus' play the middle machine, the rest o' them does t'ief bad." Kenrick walked off without saying goodbye.

Outside, Kenrick tiptoed around the masons and wet concrete to a *Play Whe* gambling booth Baljan's family managed. The booth was simply a recess in the wall covered with tinted glass and swamped with posters of Chinese caricatures. There was an unusually large chart with a history of past winning numbers. Kenrick retrieved a play slip from a wall shelf littered with crumpled paper, broken pencils and a knife, and strumming his lips with his forefinger he studied a poster of a Chinese man annotated with thirty-six *marks* (icons colloquially named). Two men who had heard of the Boxing Day race and couldn't contain their excitement suddenly appeared.

"Wha's the *mark*?" one asked, still holding Kenrick's hand and patting his shoulder. "You still min'ing *7*?"

Kenrick jerked his hand away. "You too blasted fas'."

"You and all," the other man argued with his companion, "how you go ask the man that? Kenrick is a big boy now, not a lil pipsqueak like you. You better say sorry." Before leaving, the men promised to spread the news in Dinsley Village.

Relieved and smiling, Kenrick tapped on the tinted glass while peeping through a cluster of three holes with one eye closed; from any angle only Baljan's mother's neck and bosom showed. Baljan's mother didn't hear him the first time. "Give me seven scratch and a hundred dollars on *19*!" he shouted to no avail. Muttering, Kenrick went to the shelf, snatched up a yellow pencil, sharpened it using the knife and shaded "*19*" and "*Both*" signifying the midday and evening draw. Still fuming, he shoved his play slip and money through a lattice to Baljan's mother; it disappeared as if a dog had snatched it. Inside, an online machine whirred and beeped then Baljan's mother passed Kenrick an electronic ticket. "Where m' seven scratch?" he shouted twice. Kenrick pocketed his *Play Whe* ticket and scratch cards and walked home, telling everyone he met about the race.

John Boy was *mucking out GoFast's* stall, shovelling dung into a bucket. Kenrick whisked open the hammock closest to the backyard and *steupsed* at the coins, leather straps and buckles inside. He reclined and adjusted his head and torso until comfortable. One leg stretched out in the hammock, the other on the dirt floor, he propelled the hammock then his pushing leg came up and extended over the other. Initially, on the upswing, his right shoulder bumped into the earthen *chulha* stove beside him but then his momentum slowed and was pleasant. Kenrick dug in his pocket for the scratch cards. He also found a matchstick; exploring his left ear, he lifted his buttocks and felt around for a coin. He scratched the first card–nothing. Cursing, he crumpled and stuffed it back into his pocket.

"Where *GoFast*?" he shouted, startling John Boy who spun around, mopped his forehead and said, "*GoFast*? She grazing in the savannah." Then frowning, "Boss, don't mind me saying bu' you sitting on m' bridle."

"Bu' how you soun'ing upset so?" Kenrick dragged the bridle from beneath him. "Boy, jus' go and ge' the damn horse!" Kenrick flung John Boy's *makeshift* bridle on the dirt floor and scratched the remaining cards, enjoying the torpor, the solitude, the coin's cold comfort, the grating sound against the coating that fell away like metallic dust. One by one he crumpled the cards and shoved them into his pocket. John Boy returned leading *GoFast* and shouldering a bundle of grass. Using the hammock's rope, Kenrick hoisted himself to his feet.

"I have good news, John Boy, good news!"

John Boy glared between *GoFast's* bridle lying on the ground and Kenrick. "What; that my bridle still in one piece?"

"Watch your tone, boy, before you get bad news and two hot slaps."

John Boy apologised.

"Now stand before me oh noble steed and jockey... shorts."

"Yes boss." John Boy marched up beside *GoFast* and stamped to attention.

"*Me*," Kenrick said and he began drumming his chest, "*GoFast*," his drumming quickened, "and *you*," climaxed and suddenly stopped, "in a big race."

John Boy squinted sceptically then his eyes widened. "A race, boss? Really? How?"

"You doh study how nah, I have my connections."

John Boy nodded. "Where the race will be?"

"In Santa Rosa!" Kenrick mimicked a slot machine paying out coins.

"Yes!" John Boy whooped. "Yes, yes, yes!" He congratulated *GoFast* with a vigorous rub then reached out to hug his boss.

"Enough of tha' shit," Kenrick said.

"What colours she riding in?" John Boy asked in a wounded voice.

"I thinking about red, like lucky sevens." Kenrick stroked his chin. "Lucky Sevens; bu' wait, that would o' be a good name for *GoFast*."

John Boy picked up the bridle he had made from belt buckles and leather straps. "*GoFast* could use this for the race?"

"You stupid or what? We have to be professional." He grabbed the bridle and inspected it, like a child glancing over a broken toy. "Waste o' time."

"You for real, Kenrick?" John Boy asked.

"Kenrick? Who the hell y'u calling Kenrick?"

"Sorry boss. Wha' number I riding in?"

"T'irty six."

"Why thirty six, boss?"

"Because you 's a jackass." Chuckling, Kenrick went on to describe how he'd go about acquiring the required gear; he knew a big boy who worked in a sports store.

A whistle from out front caught Kenrick's attention and lured him to the roadway. The crowd had at least one hundred people. Everyone knew about the race and they all felt festive. *This one* clutched two ducks by the neck; *that one* toted a ring-stove; Baljan wagged the rum; and *the other* carried oil, pepper and seasonings in a plastic bag. They cleared a space on the ground below the shed for cooking. The earthen *chulha* was cleaned, newspaper set ablaze and shoved between wooden chips, and a fire coaxed. The shed smelled like pepper and curry. Amidst the smoke and noise a woman said, "crack the seal," and drinks flowed. People danced with *Go-Fast*.

In the days that followed, news of the race spread like wildfire. Kenrick shot from laughing stock to regional hero. Villagers invited him to parties and John Boy soon knew rum; Baljan even fed *GoFast* Guinness. After two weeks of revelling, Kenrick established a training schedule. Next day he woke in time for lunch, drank a *reviver* (a cold beer) and nourished *GoFast* with six, hot Guinness. He pushed *GoFast* and John Boy hard and towards evening he visited *Goldwood Racing Pool*. One afternoon, on an overhead television, a favourite of his, *Mloc Trebmi*, refused to leave the gates; thus Kenrick concluded that *GoFast* required such practice.

Two weeks later, Kenrick sped his father's van to the industrial estate in Macoya. At an appliance factory he negotiated with the facilities manager, an old man with two or three teeth, who finally conceded and gave him five refrigerator boxes and a dozen cardboard flats for free. Back home his father's van stalled for gas beneath the shed. While *GoFast* stood at the edge of her stall looking on, Kenrick unloaded the van, juxtaposed the boxes like upright coffins and stepped back; they looked like starting gates without doors. Pleased,

Kenrick lay in a hammock and waited impatiently for John Boy.

When John Boy arrived at lunchtime Kenrick lifted his hands in disgust and said, "Jackass, you go now look to reach?"

"Oh gosh boss, don't talk to me so *nah*. I sorry—"

"Look boy!" Kenrick stood suddenly, bringing the hammock up with him and holding it between his legs. "I don't want to hear y'u' shit! Bring a knife from the kitchen and on top the chest o' drawers have some twine."

Working under Kenrick's strict instructions, John Boy put the refrigerator boxes to lie bottom up, stuck the knife through one corner, sliced along the length and breadth so when the boxes were upright again the flaps he had cut opened like doors.

"Good," Kenrick said. "Now *chap* off a lil bit from the top and bottom so it will look like a batwing. *Steups*, you know wha' I talking about, boy, the saloon doors like wha' it does have in them westerns."

After John Boy had converted the five refrigerator boxes into starting gates, he pierced a hole in each door and holding the knife between his teeth ran nylon through the hole and knotted it. He passed the nylon cluster to Kenrick who grabbed his shoulder and jerked him backwards. Smiling at John Boy, Kenrick yanked the gates open.

"Well done John Boy; well done!" he said, gazing through the gates at the shed, the van beneath it and the road beyond. "Your job will be to get *GoFast* inside the middle gate."

"Boss it might be easier if she think it have horses besides she."

"True," Kenrick said and removed his arm from John Boy, "but unimportant. Wha' we need is some help."

Kenrick gave John Boy brisk instructions to walk around Dinsley Village and collect as many male villagers as he could. Meanwhile Kenrick dressed in Baljan's khaki suit and red tie, sat in a hammock and shaped five cardboard horses with long necks like giraffes. When John Boy returned with a dozen or so heads, Kenrick ordered *GoFast* "nourished" and saddled.

Before leaving for the savannah Kenrick fetched his mother's bell from the dining table and allocated the people he liked least to tote the cardboard gates and flats. The sun burned hot and dust clouds puffed up and waltzed across the patchworks of green and brown. Everyone chattered excitedly except Kenrick. Holding her reins he led *GoFast* and his followers along a track, over a broken down bridge that passed over a smelly canal and around a cricket pitch covered with bamboo branches.

To the north, where the savannah met the pavement, a group of old timers and a lonesome sculptor, who was chiselling and hammering a block of wood across his knees, sat along a step-up shaded by woody trees planted along the border. The pavement bustled with uniformed students. Beyond them, cars and maxis, striped red and white like candy, zipped past on the bus route while traffic crawled along the main road. Then, as if it all happened at the same moment, someone shouted, heads turned and people pointed at *GoFast*. Kenrick smiled and jogged *GoFast* to the pavilion which was empty except for a woman sitting three rows up out of the sun's reach: The Horse Guru. She wore a white business suit with matching accessories. There was a pencil tucked behind her ear. She smiled with John Boy but regarded Kenrick and *GoFast* with professional scepticism.

"Wha' you doing here?" Kenrick shouted. He rolled his shoulders as if winding up his chest and looking back and forth over his shoulders at the dozen or so men behind him, he sniggered, "Like she come back for she uncle saddle, like she want a cattle boil in she eye again." But he gulped and jumped behind John Boy when The Horse Guru dashed down the steps and necked up to the group. She stooped and inspected *GoFast's* left foreleg.

"I'm here on assignment to watch your horse train although she looks more like a jade, my goodness. I'm a journalist, remember?"

"Journalist?" Kenrick queried, peeping over John Boy's shoulder. A smile crossed his face then suddenly broadened. He stepped into the open and craned his neck. "Wait, you mean you want to interview me?"

"Oh no-no-no Kenrick, I'm here to review *GoFast*."

"Y'u hear tha', fellars? She want to interview a horse! You ever hear damn *stupidness* so? *GoFast* cyar even talk!"

"Bu' she could drink Guinness like a bitch!" someone blurted and Kenrick cursed.

"Let's cut to the chase," The Horse Guru said, removing the pencil from behind her ear. "You do your job, I do mine."

"Look," Kenrick said but The Horse Guru had already turned for the pavilion. She climbed four rows, ironed behind her pants with her palms and sat. Tapping her teeth with the pencil she waited while Kenrick glared at her.

"Fellars," Kenrick cackled. He cleared his throat and tried mightily hard to ignore The Horse Guru. "Sometimes horses does stick in the starting gates."

"Wha' you re'lly trying to say, Kenrick?" The sculptor had left his block of wood, chisel and hammer on the pavement and joined the group. His nickname was Stallion. He was tall, bulky, red like a sorrel and had chipped teeth.

Kenrick shoved his mother's bell in Stallion's face. "What I trying to say is you should shut your damn mouth and listen." When the laughter subsided Kenrick described the training procedure to the scrum of villagers. John Boy mounted *GoFast*. Villagers arranged the cardboard gates parallel to the orange-roofed pavilion. While they worked the crowd thickened.

It took a lot of tugging and shoving to get *GoFast* into the middle box. She whinnied and stamped and kicked unconscious a man who slapped her rump. When a *Snowcone Man* gathered among the crowd, John Boy dismounted, purchased a snowcone and holding *GoFast's* bridle, with two men guiding her from the rear, he teased her through the middle gate. Standing with his back to The Horse Guru, Kenrick laughed and applauded; women clapped; men stuck fingers in their mouths and whistled; children looked up at the adults and giggled. John Boy scrambled back into the saddle, Kenrick ordered four men including Stallion into the starting gates on either side of *GoFast*. A villager distributed the cardboard horse heads, the gates closed and Kenrick assigned Baljan as the door opener.

"Jockey Shorts ready?" Kenrick shouted.

John Boy lay flat on *GoFast*, hugging her neck with his legs and head jammed against the gate. "Yes boss!"

"Jackasses ready?"

"Yes Kenrick!" chorused the four men waiting on cardboard horses inside their individual gates.

"Baljan ready?"

Baljan stood opposite Kenrick, holding the cluster of nylon attached to the gates. "Yes Ken–"

Kenrick clanged his mother's bell, Baljan yanked the gates open, and four men, straddling Kenrick's cardboard carvings, dashed from their gates screaming "Giddy-up!" and whooping like Apaches.

"False start; false start!" Kenrick shouted but Stallion galloped nonstop to the savannah's southern end. Laughing, the other "riders" returned to their gates but all eyes narrowed with silent determination when Kenrick rebuked them. All around spectators had doubled over laughing for during this commotion *GoFast* and John Boy never moved.

Kenrick organised another race. From the sidelines he raised his mother's bell. The crowd leaned forward and waited. In the pavilion The Horse Guru crossed her legs and hunched over. The bell rang and horses, both real and make believe, lurched out, *GoFast* taking along the refrigerator box so she and John Boy looked like a giant milk carton with four legs. After five lengths the milk carton fell with a thud and Stallion won the race. Kenrick cursed. Kenrick rang the bell. Kenrick reprimanded John Boy.

"You have a mad man winning!" he shouted. "Y'u ain't shame?"

Disgusted, he ordered the middle gate removed so four boxes remained, two on either side with a space in between for *GoFast*. A volunteer from the crowd held up a cardboard flat to keep *GoFast* in line. The four men riding the cardboard horses got into position. Kenrick set the race. The crowd waited. The bell rang, the volunteer dropped the flat and *Go-Fast* thundered to a win, earning relieved, comical applause as if the spectators meant to say: we always knew she could do it.

"You see! You see!" Kenrick shouted, running up to Stallion and when he had caught up, he laughed spitefully in his face. "Y'u los', y'u flipping mad bitch, y'u los'!" But Stallion, flapping his face, neighing and snorting, returned to the starting gates. Because *GoFast* breezed through the other races Kenrick didn't notice when The Horse Guru left. But the following week she showed every day. Kenrick scorned her.

Besides The Horse Guru, Kenrick had another problem. He had the horse, he had the jockey and he had the equipment but he didn't have money for gambling, and *GoFast's* odds were 30 to 1. The good news was that *GoFast* now thrilled Dinsley so Kenrick solicited donations but most villagers had other Christmas commitments. Naturally, Kenrick took his wild, money-spinning ideas to businessmen. Baljan's father was one of these businessmen. They talked at length then came to a verbal agreement.

"You want half the money up front?" Baljan's father asked. "I could pu' it in the slot machine for you and we call it square."

"No, I want cash," Kenrick said, working his ear with a matchstick. "This money is for a big bet."

That Friday, after Baljan's father paid off Kenrick and added a case of Guinness for *GoFast's* nourishment, Kenrick, *GoFast* and John Boy visited the bar; and for every bottle of rum a customer purchased they earned a *"complimentary"* ride on the famous horse. The venture scored. Other bar owners formed contracts with Kenrick, and *The GoFast Campaign*, powered by Guinness, laboured on, a superb period in Dinsley.

Instead of heading home after these parties, Kenrick and John Boy rode *GoFast* to the Dinsley Savannah and rested, owner and jockey propped against the horse, hands clasped behind their heads, giggling like school girls and *seeing* their Boxing Day win. And so it went, on and on, night after night. After a Christmas party, the trio stumbled to the savannah. Lying in dewy grass and watching the black, starry blanket above, Kenrick trembled with pride and excitement; he felt no tiredness.

"You could imagine winning this thing, John Boy? Because I feeling it!"

"Gosh boss, the more you talk about it the more better it does sound," John Boy slurred. Kenrick pointed at a shooting star and although John Boy hadn't seen it, he closed his eyes and wished upon it. "When I win my mother go be re'l proud o' me."

Kenrick shot to his feet and slipped on a Guinness bottle he had left behind the night before. He launched the bottle with all his might towards the priority bus route where it shattered, loud enough for *GoFast* to cock her ears. Hands on hips he faced John Boy.

"You thinking small. Imagine what this race could do for me, wha' it could do for we! Watch wha' it do for Dinsley! You think is Christmas tha' have everybody excited? I's me! Winning will put *me*, you, everybody on the map!"

"What about *GoFast*?" John Boy asked.

"This race bigger than *GoFast* now. Tha' damn horse is just the way out o' all this *stupidness*, like '*Manure on the outside!*'

or '*Two-two Brains*!' Remember how people laugh in the beginning? No more rides for small money! Humph! I doesn't fo'get."

"What about her? You still love she?" John Boy sat up, folded his legs, began stroking *GoFast*. "*Ent GoFast, ent* Kenrick don't love you no more?"

"I's only 'bout the race now," Kenrick scoffed. "I's like this… I could never feel tha' lil boy *thing* you have for *GoFast*. Tha' is the difference between men and boys, wo'k and play, surviving and having a mother to feed you' lazy ass."

"And wha' going and happen to *GoFast* after the race, boss?"

"Well… this is between me and you – don't mind Baljan and a few other people know – I bet three thousand dollars on *GoFast* at different racing pools." Kenrick searched the darkness as if awaiting some revelation. "She odds is 30 to 1 so y'u done know wha' tha' mean. I bet all tha' money on a *win*."

"Three thousand dollars? Tha' money could o' use fo' pellets to boost *GoFast*!"

"The Guinness is to boost *GoFast*!" Kenrick shouted. He relaxed. "Look, after the *win* I going Las Vegas, plus I want a motorbike. I's time to redefine and refine Kenrick."

John Boy stopped stroking *GoFast* and smelled his hands. "My mother want to know wha' in it fo' me."

An icy wind whooshed over the savannah. Kenrick turned to the east from whence it had come then frowned at John Boy, kicked his worn sole and said, "Don't worry, I will handle you."

"And… wha' if we lose?"

"Shoot man! This negative talk! I don't like it!" Kenrick swore: "If we lose – and we not going to lose; I mean, oh gosh man, people might start calling me *Shit for Brains* – I will give you *GoFast*!"

"Really? But boss… it ain't a penny to mind a horse. As it is *GoFast* will eat anything!"

Kenrick winced. "You thinking crap now," he said and kicked grass. "Watch this! Watch this!" he shouted and stood with his legs apart, clapping and striking his chest in quick succession so the rhythm thundered like a horse galloping over firm ground. "This! This is the sound of *GoFast* winning. This is why I bet all my money on *GoFast*." He quit his antics suddenly and kicked John Boy. "Enough of y'u' crap! Come le' we go and sleep!"

On Boxing Day, villagers rose an hour before daylight. Even enemies said good morning to each other. Men, women and children rushed about, calling out to each other, querying the racetrack's dress code. People chattered with excitement. *This one* promised he'd sponsor three or four ducks; *that one* agreed she'd bring the roti; Baljan confirmed he'd bring drinks; and *the other* would cook a chicken "*bunje* down with plenty pepper!" Even the village drunkards bobbed with excitement.

Amidst all this excitement, Kenrick felt like Santa Claus, standing barebacked in front his mud house, brushing his teeth, probing his ear with a matchstick and spitting foam in the canal. The savannah lay empty; neither cricket nor kite-flying played in anyone's mind. Three or four houses away, Samo and Nat, members of *The Dinsley All Stars*, squatted around a fire burning in the road, adjusting the pitch on their *tassas* (kettle drums). People bustled around Kenrick and depending on how he felt, he shooed them or addressed their concerns. The man whom *GoFast* had kicked unconscious brought Kenrick the previous day's newspaper. On the second to last page The Horse Guru had labelled *GoFast* "a green horse; no chance". Kenrick said, "She blasted colour-blind; *GoFast* brown." He rolled up the newspaper and held it up like a sword. "Gone from here nah!" he barked. Smiling, he threw the paper in the canal. Supporters came and went. "Wear red!" heralds shouted, "Kenrick wa' everybody to wear red!"

Kenrick shaved and showered in the outdoor bathroom then went into his bedroom. His towel went on a nail behind the door. Working in front the wardrobe mirror with the idea many visitors would soon come, he doused his face and body with aftershave. Beyond his reflection, past curtains stuck through louvers, Kenrick monitored John Boy who was grooming *GoFast* into respectability with a scrubbing brush. Kenrick scoffed and rolled up his socks. The soiled-clothes basket had all his underwear. "Today is my day to shine!" he said and did something unthinkable. He slipped on cuffed black pants, zipped up cautiously, viewed his bum in the mirror. His butt crack showed. Satisfied, he struggled into a red turtleneck and red satin jacket. The jacket rested comfortably on his shoulders but the sleeves stopped short of his wrists and were tight around the armpits so he couldn't raise his hands higher than his shoulders. Kenrick smiled and doused his clothes with aftershave. After drying his hands, he flung his towel in a corner. The gel and comb lay on the dresser, crowded by gambling slips, coins and matchsticks. Hunched over, he styled his hair into a *wicked* side part and slid the comb in his breast pocket. He practised retrieving it.

Squinting, he blew a kiss at the mirror, pointed two guns at himself and said, "Yes Indian, y'u shining like a shilling!" He peered through the back window. "John Boy, that is enough! Stop brushing my horse."

"Yes boss, okay boss, I only talking to *GoFast* boss."

"You finish nourishing she?"

"Yes boss, twenty four Guinness in all boss. Two bucket just like you say."

"Good, now go and get y'u' ass ready. Your colours in my mother bedroom. Go fas' before you make me late."

John Boy removed his jersey and clipped it to a clothesline supported by a bamboo rod. He went to the barrel beside *GoFast's* stall and splashed water on his face and beneath his arms. He dried with his dirty jersey.

Meanwhile Kenrick went to his parents' room and waited for John Boy whose riding boots were next to *GoFast's* new saddle and bridle, both the colour of red sand. The saddle cloth was opened on the bed. On top were John Boy's matching *silks*, whip and jockey helmet. When John Boy entered, he clutched his mouth and gasped.

"I dump the bridle you make because these thing here is better thing," Kenrick said, frowning at John Boy. "Doh twist up y'u' face like that, y'u riding with a good number."

John Boy picked up his *silks* and held it open at the sleeves. "This is a good number?" On the back, written in white, was numeral seven.

"For slot machines yeah, in *Play Whe* no," Kenrick said. "Listen, we leaving in two minutes. When you ready go outside and wait for me."

"Yes boss!"

Kenrick re-entered his room, stood on the bed and felt around on top the wardrobe for his gambler's spray. He drenched his clothes and rubbed behind his ears.

"Like a big shot!" he said to the mirror. "Like a winner!"

John Boy knocked and entered Kenrick's room adjusting his crotch and riding helmet which was too big for his head. "Right boss, I finish. How y'u' boy looking? Talk your mind."

"Tu'n 'round le' me see… like a re'l ass," Kenrick smirked. "Don't worry, seven is a good number. Now go outside and in a few minutes time start shouting my name." Kenrick waited inside until the chanting began and when it had escalated to that of a legion, he stepped outside and grinned modestly at the crowd's thunderous applause.

"Alright-alright, tha's enough." He subdued the noise with facedown palms. "Le' we go. We have a race to win!"

Villagers crammed into cars and as Kenrick's father's van had no gasoline, the entourage, led by *GoFast*, crawled three noisy miles east to the racetrack as Kenrick and John Boy smiled and waved. At the racetrack Kenrick dismounted and grasped John Boy's heel.

"Today we going to make history, boy. You win this race for me and me and you is friend for life!"

"Yes boss!" John Boy snapped back with a toothy grin of determination.

Kenrick adjusted his jacket with a shoulder roll. "How I looking?"

"The red take you re'l good boss."

Kenrick slapped John Boy on the leg. "Do *whatever* it takes to win." He tugged *GoFast's* new bridle until the horse faced him. "And you! Run like the devil behind y'u!"

Kenrick turned for the stands and smiled broadly as it came alive: that sea of indistinguishable faces, shielding their eyes and scanning outfield as if a race was in progress; helium balloons on strings; *nuts men*; vendors shouldering racks framed with blue and pink cotton candy and shouting bawdy slogans; a tricycle fitted with a beach umbrella and icebox and the *Snowcone Man...*

Feeling larger than life, Kenrick goaded, "You still selling *snowcone*? Gi'e me one with condense' milk, I feeling like a big shot today!"

Kenrick swaggered towards the finish line, ignoring familiar whistles and shouts from Dinsley village folk; they'd tarnish his reputation as a horse owner. A young photographer stopped him for pictures. A breathless monotone cackled over Santa Rosa's public address system:

"Allowance race coming up, *Septet* running for *Gerard Stables*, 2 to 1 odds, a lovely horse folks and I know it since I once mounted her mother. Running at 30 to 1, maiden horse *GoFast*, owned by Mr. Kenrick *Maharaj* – sorry, that's Maraj – of Dinsley."

Villagers roared and whistled as colourful horses cantered to the starting gates. I will go to the VIP lounge in a moment, Kenrick thought, propped against the rails, spellbound by his *snowcone*, relishing crimson syrup on ice, thick condensed milk – sweet, almost fruity, maybe acidic, a bit seductive, no, almost done, yes, definitely *moreish* – its taste fascinating the boy trapped inside; when the starting gates lurched open, Kenrick flung his *snowcone*.

GoFast shot from her gate leaving *Septet*, a sorrel and the favourite, in a mocking dust cloud.

In the stands, people jostled for a better view. *The Dinsley All Stars* burst into song. Cymbals and whistles joined and on cue *tassas* erupted like machineguns. The crowd went wild; fists punched the sky and rasp screams urged *GoFast* on.

The horses thundered around the first bend–then the second. When *Septet* inched past *GoFast* the crowd fell silent. On the final stretch John Boy dug his heels into *GoFast* and shouted "Ya! Ya!"

GoFast pushed ahead.

At the finish line Kenrick ripped off his red jacket and turtleneck; one hand held up his pants just below his bare buttocks, the other waved his clothes in wild anticipation. Kenrick lusted given *GoFast's* odds of 30 to 1. He had counted on winning and here *his GoFast* came, down the final stretch, *his* jockey now flogging her like an irate teacher.

"*No chance? Steups!* What y'u have to say now, eh Miss Guru?" Kenrick cupped his mouth and screamed: "Go faster!"

Suddenly *GoFast* stopped.

The move flung John Boy from her back and over the finish line; the cheering stopped but resumed when *Septet* shot past *GoFast* and won the race.

GoFast couldn't be bothered. While Kenrick kicked and cursed she gobbled his unfinished *snowcone*.

Swift

In Trinidad every village have two things in common: a recreation ground and at least one or two *pipers*. Like Tonto, he is a piper. He does pick up beer bottles and wipe tables in a rumshop, and collect he pay in drinks. Irish is a piper too. Every morning he does sweep the canal in front Ms. Joanne shop just so he could eat a aloo pie. And le' me don't talk about Sparky, because everybody in St. Helena already know how he get that name.

But me? You have to understand me. I is a opportunist. Like everybody else, I understand spending power. That does separate the junkie from the drinker. I is a man on the move, hungry for money but not a beggar, hungry for rum but not an alcoholic. A piper don't get pay because he don't work. So you can't call me that. I does work! And I does get pay. Anything you have to do I doing but paper mus' pass. People does want to take advantage of me, and you know what? To some extent I does let them. Once they pay for it, because people, especially woman with lazy husbands, have a kind of way they like to feel they in charge. It might not be much, but you must pay me; even if is a dolla' self. So, unlike them other pipers, I is a bright fellar because I don't sleep in a recreation ground and I have a salary.

Time does fly like salary, yes. A year ago I was hustling, busting my tail, picking up paper 'roun' man yard for lil twenty five cents and cutting acre of grass fo' twenty dollars. People mus' be does feel I is a cocaine specialist, but tha's not my vice. I like cigarette and, father lord, I love rum. Things change when I get a contract wo'k with a respectable oil company that does fuel plane going place like London and America, where all my family uses to go when they was alive. They dead now, thank goodness for small mercies, that wicked, *dutty* bunch of people. Anyway, I drifting from the story. The rum does cause that so bear with me.

Yes, so, I get this work, right, and I was basically doing the same thing with little extra duties on the side, like washing car and tending to a place called the tank farm, although I never see no goat or cow minding there. The fellars on work re'l like me, especially Shades, one black bitch who always eating, but never have money; and so he like to boast and say how he have ten cheque book full up with deposits. All the employees like that. Don't talk 'bout the one who start to ride motorbike the other day. He worse than a piper. He does be so broken, he does ask me for money. Anyways, one morning after I t'ief a smoke, the foreman, Andy, a short neck Indian fellar with a fancy glasses, broach me:

"Swift, it having a drill a little later; company procedure. I want you to participate."

"Wha' it have in it for me?" I say. I don't really like Andy head. Anytime I check him for holidays he does blank me, and I have fourteen days inside.

Andy watch me over he glasses. "Swift, it's part of your job."

"To hell with that! I not participating."

Andy dip in he shirt jack and pull out a twenty dollars. My mind done wo'king overtime. Tha's a nip of rum and a chaser. He tear the money in half and tell me after the drill, when I finish wash he car, I go get the next piece.

"Swift, you have to be professional. It's a fire drill so pretend you're burnt badly. Make it as real as possible! *Act good!*"

I watching Andy *cut eye*, still vex 'bout the twenty and only halfway interested, but when he say *act* he catch me. I always wanted to be in a movie.

"I will handle it!" I say and lef' Andy standing right there.

Lunch time I wo'king in the blazing sun when a siren gone off. Drill start! I out a cigarette I was smoking and make a dash for where the trucks park up 'long the fence. Employees running around like is a re'l action movie. I run out in the yard, waving my hand, like I stopping a plane, and bawling:

"Oh gorm! I on fire! Save me! Save me! Oh gorm, I go dead!" My hand them spread out eagle but them workers not taking me seriously. I drop on the ground and start to roll. "Oh gorm! Out me! Out me!"

A fire truck blazing sirens pull up; I still rolling. One big Creole run out, holding a fire extinguisher like a gun, and my mind run on Jim because he promise me a small change if I get one for him – not a Creole, a fire extinguisher. Anyways, I say:

"Creole, out me! Out me! I on fire! I go dead!" Well the fellar confused and only looking 'roun' while man deading on the ground. I say: "Boy, out me fas', I have rum to drink. Wha' happen, boy, you 'fraid or what?"

The Creole blood ge' hot because y'u know *negro* fellars don't like when you call them *boy*, not even if is Trini parlance.

"Who you calling *boy*? Eh? Y'u licey head Indian!"

And he start to act. If you see action! Foam fo' so in me backside! I rolling on the ground with me hand stretch out, like I going and make a big dive. Foam all in my eye. I see Andy running, he belly flapping like a accordion.

"Swift, what happened?" He sounding worried so I know I acting good.

"Andy? Oh gosh, is you, boy? Me life flashing before me eyes. I dying. I ge' bu'n up!"

"Swift, we have to get you to the hospital!" If you hear he voice how fine, it only shattering like he eat a harmonica. The fellar was re'lly worried. I acting along. I see a set of faces over me, Shades and all there, roti in one hand, cheque book in the nex'. I covered in foam, and m' eye bu'ning. Another fireman run up and they throw me on a stretcher. They shove me in a ambulance, and is speed like that to Arima Hospital. Whole drive I only moaning and groaning and they only cussing me to stop, but that was all part o' the thing.

The greatest is them fellars drop me in Arima Hospital and leave me on the stretcher soak down in foam. I say is all part o' the plan. I start to bawl again. They hustle me into Casualty. When a chicken-face doctor (who have a patch of hair on he Adam's apple and looking like he buy he licence) atten' to me I pu' on a damn good show. Two nurses take me pressure.

The doc was a good actor. "This patient is critical!" Then he ask wha' I does usually take when I sick.

"Salt, lime, black pepper and Puncheon."

"You need sick leave?" He all businesslike and he long nose almost touching the paper he writing on.

I say, "With pay?"

"Of course!"

"While I on this sick leave I could drink rum?"

"You want to?" he ask and cross something off.

"Why not?" The two nurses looking between me and the doc like they smelling something bad. I tell the Creole one to watch the next way.

"Okay, no antibiotics." He make a next scratch, jot something down and hand me a sick leave certificate. "You're free to go."

I wipe foam from 'roun' me eye. "Thank you, Dr. Lal."

I walk from Arima to Piarco bathe down in foam. Andy shift was just finishing. When he see me, he turtle neck stick out a lil more than usual. I dip my hand in he pocket, pull out the *other* half o' the twenty and hand him my sick leave.

I drink rum for two weeks.

Schooldays

Sometimes when I doing the government wo'k, painting pebbles and tree trunks white or brush cutting grass on the side o' the road, I does think about school and although I doesn't remember much I does miss it. One Monday morning meh wacker hit a stone. The stone fly through a hole in the canvas barrier two woman was holding up on the pavement and break a car glass. While I hol'ing meh head, bawling, a fellar I know from secondary school come out the car. He wearing shirt and tie and a gold watch that only sliding down to his elbow. He holding a lil boy's hand. After he and the foreman argue about who have to pay for the damages, me and he stand up under an almond tree and he show me a business card, pointing at letters that bigger than his name and explaining to me how he have three degree and a NBA in business administration and journalism and was working on a third book named *Boy Days.*

When he finally ge' fed up about talking about himself and I get fed up of listening to him talk about himself, he introduce me to his son and we start to talk about junior sec: who

have big wo'k, who married, who dead from AIDS or in accident. The talk was going so sweet the lil boy say he want to
hear about everything, because we schooldays sound like real
old time days, where people used to pitch marble and play
scooch and go dollar jam the Friday before carnival. I laugh and
say, small man, we younger than that, then his father take
over the conversation. He say:

I often reflect on my schooldays and I fantasise. And fantasise. Despite this I'm not certain I'd return to secondary
school, but I envy school boys when I see them. They should
be greedy for their schooldays for there is nothing in this
world as important as education and the opportunity will
never come around again. And in a few twinkles, their memories will weaken and looking at themselves in the mirror, they
will ponder days so distant and surreal they'll wonder if they
ever existed; especially if they did poorly at exams and work
dead-end jobs in the public sector. You see these memories,
relative to the individual, are queer, for they are both delight-
ful and lethargic; one cannot help but believe that *their*
schooldays were most magnificent and incomparable. I do.

You talk re'l sense there, I say.

Quite recently my fantasies rekindled, he say, pulling his
gold watch back down to his wrist. You see, I encountered
another classmate – he isn't doing too well, works as a health
inspector – an obnoxious but sentimental lad, who flipped
open his wallet and showed me a group photograph therein. I
was in the picture! I couldn't believe my eyes for I was but a
boy. Behind us was the school, built on tropical land and
shadowed by mountains, but fenced like a prison. Along the
perimeter were poui trees which students sat beneath and
crossed their legs; some for solitude; others for laughs; cou-

ples for romance when yellow flowers warned of April exams. A useless tennis court was next to the car park and further down, a hairy savannah used for sports, but mostly football.

In another picture the study blocks, north of the savannah, stood in tandem like three milk cartons. There was a cafeteria also, which served expensive, tasteless food, apart from its beef pies – small, spicy and flaky. Every morning, when the bell rang, students rushed from the cafeteria and queued in an assembly hall. Latecomers who didn't escape punishment swept this hall during lunch and again after school. After the national anthem, school pledge and a prayer by the commissioned form, the students of Form 1:5 would trudge to Block A as if it were penance; and it was penance for, except for a syllabus, schooldays were unstructured with no clear motive, little moral value and a cast of way too many characters.

There was Martin – you remember Martin, right? – a thin, tall, greedy boy; a spectacle with his pop star pants and white socks. At the bell, he would fly – up, up, up – to the Home Economics block to pilfer lunches, evading the prefects squinting over distribution. When the caterers supplied roti, pumpkin and curried mango, Martin dodged Mrs. Charles's iron stare behind stacks of boxes and returned for seconds.

There was George, a grimy, chubby lad with puppy eyes, unforgiving acne and a special eye for skinny girls. He lived with his grandfather and hadn't seen his mother in thirteen years; she *made up* by mailing her love each month in cardboard barrels containing America's trendiest fashions. On Thursdays, George wore *old school* sneakers.

George and Jean-Pierre were ring-on-finger buddies. Jean-Pierre was a stout, adult-sized chap with an angel face and a fighter's heart. Everyone knew George hung out with him because of his muscles, but their friendship ended in form three after Jean-Pierre punched George square in his face and broke his glasses. It's a complicated story, involving new characters, so hold on to your socks:

It started when a boy named Wazim paid another named Fat Pete (tall and clumsy with tiny teeth that made his lips seem enormous) five dollars to clobber Christian because he had pulled Stacey's plaits. Fat Pete agreed because except for bus tickets, his mother never gave him anything to take to school. So he struck Christian, his best friend, with a splendid right hook for Wazim had offered ten dollars for a sucker punch.

Christian cussed and a fight erupted. It was nowhere as vicious as the battle between Jean-Pierre and *Ugly Brigo*, but word traversed the halls, relayed by students wishing to bear the news *first*. In a flash, a hostile audience cheered from behind the shutters, as chairs and tables flew across the room in super slow motion. Christian sank his foot into Pete's stomach, sparking cheers among the crowd.

In the middle of the fight, Ms. Sahadeo, a puny Spanish teacher, showed up, but her feeble attempts to simmer things went unheard, so she rushed to the staff room to fetch someone bigger. The fight ended when the Vice Principal appeared. His name was Mr. Roach, a man with a menacing stride, whiskers for eyebrows, a massive baldhead that sloped into piercing eyes, and a sharp, sonorous voice for barking students' surnames. He possessed a whip, *Suzie*, wrapped with tape at either end, which he brandished like a wand.

"Hello-hello-hello! Seenath! Procope! Acres! What's going on up there?" he barked, and to the scampering crowd, "Get back to your classes," and to a boy adjusting his zip, "Not you, Maharaj, you wait right there!" To their surprise, the fighters escaped with a warning. "Ms. Sahadeo will administer your punishment," Mr. Roach concluded and seized Maharaj by his ears. Hidden behind shutters now, students laughed and a faint smile may have crossed Mr. Roach's face.

Ms. Sahadeo was blue vex when she returned to her Spanish class, but her face had a permanent twist, as when one is angry or constipated. She let Fat Pete off with a warning, but she found Christian to be an aleck so she demanded one thousand lines, in Spanish, for cussing. It took her one hour to settle the gossipers and when she did, the bell rang for the day. That afternoon Christian and Fat Pete walked home together, as was their habit, the latter buying and sharing soft drinks and beef pies with Wazim's money.

Christian was George's *second best friend*, so he agreed to assist with the *lines*. They secured an empty classroom and began the senseless work, George struggling to mimic Christian's cursive writing. Reinako suddenly appeared. He was a tad fatter than Martin and the second greediest boy in school. In form one, Martin and Reinako had founded the *Box Lunch Crew*, an organisation with growing membership. Reinako was always bitter, like someone had vexed his soul, but it wasn't a contemptuous bitterness, like Ms. Sahadeo's – it was more provocative.

"*Jeez-an-ages!*" he wailed. "Jean-Pierre could really pelt hard!"

"Them boys playing *scooch* nah?" grunted Christian, thinking of the net-less tennis court, which became a prison when young men gathered daily and smashed flannel balls against each other's back. "George, boy, we r-e-a-l-l-y missing out!"

139

"Who! Jean-Pierre could pelt?" George said mockingly and *steupsed*. "Boy, he's a weakling. He can't lash me."

"You brave to talk so 'bout strong man Jean-Pierre," Reinako instigated, forgetting the *scooch*, and, recalling the topical incident, winked at Christian, "Remember what he do *Ugly Brigo*?"

Christian nodded: Jean-Pierre's leather fists had made *Ugly Brigo* uglier.

"He can't come around me with his crap," George declared.

Reinako found Jean-Pierre and informed him George had branded him a faggot in a classroom packed with students. After school Jean-Pierre punched George, a calculated, effortless blow that smashed his glasses, incapacitating him for two weeks. In class they avoided each other. Christian became George's *best friend*.

When Christian delivered the lines he completed for punishment, Ms. Sahadeo tore the pages down and across then tossed them into a bin. Christian muttered a silent curse and purposed to flatten her car tyres, but never did. He had other things to think about, like science.

The four science labs were in the middle block, second floor. Each had a metal chair and desk belonging to the teacher. Students sat on wooden stools and wrote on wooden slabs running from the front to the back, where book bags were piled during class time. Experiments including the Bunsen burner were most exciting.

Months passed before Form 3:5 acquired a Biology teacher, a thin, nerdy, fearsome East Indian man, with unruly hair and enormous spectacles, who wore his pants just below his chest. His name was Mr. Ramnath, a stickler with a vile tongue, accurate aim and a special eye for his East Indian students. He liked to toss dusters across the class; Delano, a short, stocky fellow, like Jean-Pierre, was the primary target. Delano had the face of a ruffian but was mellow and soft-spoken. Martin was Mr. Ramnath's second favourite target. He used to taunt Mr. Ramnath about his *high* pants:

"Sir, like your pants smoke weed or wha'?"

Martin was either a brave or foolish fellow. Things escalated between the two until Mr. Ramnath had Martin kneel before the blackboard, prompting Christian to laugh. Mr. Ramnath sentenced Christian to his knees, and while the biologist taught nothing, the boys blew chalk dust gathered in a sill below the blackboard at each other. Martin delighted his classmates by securing a stick of chalk and scrawling, "Ramnath is an ass," but the teacher turned at the twinkling eyes and chuckles of the other students.

"You all are behaving like pigs!" Mr. Ramnath screamed. He suspended six students, including Christian who reported at home that the Biologist had labelled them pigs.

The subsequent year students chose subjects then they were uprooted and mixed, as if ingredients for a human cake. Christian opted for Form 4:1 as it included Agriculture (a double award subject), biology and accountancy. George opted for the same, a decision he made more for his best friend, Christian, than himself. Martin followed; the agricultural block was closest to the Home Economics department. Jean-Pierre left for Form 4:5 to pursue his passion for computers. Wazim followed Stacey into the realm of science. Reinako, still provocative, didn't belong to any one class.

Form 4:1 occupied the *Agri Shed*, a capacious, one-storey block with a flat roof. To the south were rows of weedy beds and barren fruit trees, ravaged by an unsolved fire and carved with two generations of students' names; there was a proud Starch mango tree also, but beyond the fence. The shed comprised of three sections: the classroom had rows of low wooden desks and benches, designed to accommodate a pair. Next to the blackboard was a rotted table tennis board; the structure's midsection was a corridor of shelves packed with seed boxes, made as assignments, and unlabelled pesticides to the tiptop; beyond this corridor were pens, six on either side, built to house ducks and chickens, but storing farm tools arranged in no particular order. The *Agri Shed* was a most enjoyable resort, for three quarters of the time allotted to the discipline was spent outdoors. Students worked in pairs, hunched over allotments, uprooting and tossing weeds between their legs to other beds.

Familiar faces but new names came to 4:1; a nostalgic experience:

There was Jayden, a garrulous lad with a cookie's face, copper hair on his arms and head, and a madman's laugh, more hilarious and peculiar than his incomprehensible jokes.

Ronald was a dark East Indian lad with a shy, nonstop smile. He had transferred from 3:1, an all-boys class. He wore baggy pants that dragged beneath his soles. He brought his lunch wrapped in foil and after each meal he folded the wrapping into a square for use the next day. His books and bag smelled of roti, pumpkin, curry and other rich, East Indian spices.

Valentin was a local white, a wordless poster boy who charmed females of all races with his fair skin, rock star's hairdo, hazel eyes and stocky legs. Even the mothers who waited for their children on afternoons admired him. Rumour had it that two women stalked him in a car, but Valentin lived only for wrestling and "devil music."

Randy was a troubled lad transferred from another school. He walked with his head down and his fingers slung beneath his bag strap. Like Martin, he enjoyed sampling his colleagues' food and snacks, but he remained adamant about not joining the *Box Lunch Crew*. He wore enormous shoes which Jayden claimed arrived at his destinations five minutes before him, and accompanied his movements with sound effects. When he walked: "*Chik, chik, chik, chik.*" He reserved "Slap," "*Po-tow!*" and "Cuff," for when he and Valentin sparred. While looking around, he uttered a robotic, "*Er-eeek-er-eeek!*"

Nikita was also new. She had returned from the United States. Of extraordinary beauty and physique, with a Roman nose, light skin and thick, black Afro hair, she didn't care for female company and she sucked willy-nilly on her thumb.

The class had two Stephens, boys of East Indian descent, who had the same medium height and light complexion, but were the antithesis of each other. Stephen Maharaj, the son of a wealthy businessman, paraded the school with hands criss-crossing his scraggy frame. He was arrogant, hot-blooded, Gemini, with horrendous teeth, but lucky with girls, or, perhaps, his money was; nevertheless he spent his days romancing in blinded classrooms, while paid hands scanned the corridors for his nemesis, Mr. Roach.

Stephen Sankar, on the other hand, was a poor farm boy who wasted his days seated in the *Agri Shed*, with his back to the lanes of vegetables outside and his knees propped up on the bench he shared with Winston, a reticent bosom buddy. This Stephen had the queer habit of sucking willy-nilly on his left index and middle finger, with such viciousness his skin burst and bled, while twisting a lock of hair extending below his eyebrows. Otherwise, he used the desk to practise video game "combos" with an imaginary joystick and buttons. Stephen Sankar earned the nickname *Barbie* within a week, so it wasn't difficult to distinguish the two.

Krystal and Ayanna had zero in common, except for their lewd encounters with Stephen, but were best friends. Krystal was filthy rich, an obnoxious wench, who envied Nikita without reason. Ayanna was African, with high cheekbones and hair she struggled to pull back and hold together with white bubbles. She was from a single parent home and fought Krystal's battles. Nikita had thrice crushed her.

Mr. Badaga, the farm attendant, chain-smoked. He had a round, tense stomach like a drum, wore ragged office clothes and garden boots, had chest hair that stuck past his shirt, and, somehow, was always wet. He was talkative, except when he smoked, and he detested students of other disciplines. Once, when Wazim visited, Mr. Badaga offered him a cigarette, but no sooner had the hook-nosed student taken his first puff, the farm attendant collared and dragged him, begging and screaming, to Mr. Roach, laying charges of smoking in the forbidden fruit trees. A fourteen-day suspension followed, and although Stacey moved on Wazim never stopped trying to woo her.

Mr. Badaga's subordinate was his son, Mohan, who had officially changed his name to Salim Abu Muhammad, a dull, self-proclaimed jihadist, who worked hard and spent his free time canvassing for disciples. The first week of 4:1, he approached Christian and Jayden as they sowed sweet pepper seeds. He squatted on his heels, thrust a cutlass into the earth between his legs and whispered:

"Brothers, do you fear death?"

Jayden stood and laughed, but Christian became nervous. Listening, he sank his fingers into the mushy brown dirt, displacing enough soil for a two-inch hole. Then, he sprinkled sweet pepper seeds, covered the cavity and packed the earth with his thumb.

"A war is coming," Salim warned. "The West must fall."

"Who going and make a bomb?" Jayden laughed. "You?"

"I make one already."

"Where it is?" Christian asked.

Salim scanned the area. He stood and toyed with his cutlass. "I make it with garden chemicals. I make three. I want all you to go with me to bomb the West."

"When you say the West, where you mean?" Jayden queried, his eyes on Christian.

"I don't know the West good," Salim shrugged, "but anywhere beyond Port of Spain."

A loud scream ended the boys' laughter. Suddenly, Martin appeared and dashed between the vegetable rows, cussing, his pants rolled above his knees, Krystal and Ayanna chasing him.

"Tha's a pad in Krystal hand?" Christian asked.

"A-ha... yeah... a-ha-ha... and it have... a-ha-ha-ha... blood on it... a-har-har-har-har!"

"Infidels!" Salim hissed.

Martin darted for the fruit trees, Krystal pouncing behind him with an outstretched hand, but Ayanna shot across the field and as her prey zoomed past the pomerac tree, she lurched at him, her fingers brushing against his sleeves. Ayanna's impetus off-balanced her, sending her skidding, face-down on the grass and into a compost heap, but Krystal leaped over her and caught Martin who had slowed. She smeared the red sanitary pad in Martin's face. Violently then, the school fight of the century erupted: Martin versus Krystal and Ayanna. The footballers and romancers in the savannah beyond the drain swarmed the fence and cheered as the girls manhandled the *Box Lunch Crew*'s founder. But Mr. Roach's bark stalled the action:

"Hello-hello-hello! What's going on here! Ahing! You fighting again?" he said, directing his whip towards Krystal and, turning it upon Ayanna, "And you, Lewis, why you still following *this* one, even after I talk to you? Explain yourself!"

Despite it being ketchup on the pad, Mr. Roach suspended Ayanna and Krystal for one month. Martin's nickname changed from *Box Lunch Jedi-Master* to *Periods Boy*. Krystal returned to school, four months later, pregnant; Mr. Roach expelled her.

When Form Five came, everyone had forgotten about Krystal. A lot changed, including the temperament and vices of the older students. *Scooch*, basketball, cricket and football became relics passed on to younger form students, who knew nothing of raging hormones. Martin regained his reputation as *Box Lunch Jedi-Master*. Word still had it that Mr. Ramnath sexed his East Indian students. George became infatuated with Simone, and she didn't mind the attention so George abandoned his usual gang of idiotic friends. Randy, Christian, Jayden, Valentin, Ronald and Nikita no longer traversed the school during free periods, but huddled together on the table tennis board at the front of the *Agri Shed*, often times, chatting until the bell ended the torpor of the day. Salim Abu Muhammad was still stupid and scheming to bomb the West. Stacey united with Wazim. Ronald's bag still smelled of curry.

"Ronald, you don't get fed up of roti?" Christian asked during lunch one day. "Is tha' the foil from form four?"

Ronald sat, un-wrapping a sizzling, aromatic roti, stuffed with mushy pumpkin, coloured red with diced pepper. "No boy! You mad? How tha' go be the same foil? You want me dead?"

"I mean, I does get fed up of this bread, cheese and kuchela," Christian complained. "My mother making this like it going out of style."

Jayden laughed.

Nikita resumed sucking her thumb after saying, "You shush, Jayden! Your mother don't ever cook for you. You always buying food."

"Because he mother like a set of man," Christian joked.

Jayden cackled, "Ah-har-har-har."

"No but seriously, Ronald, you want to swap lunch?"

"Bread, cheese and kuchela," Randy highlighted, wiping his chin, and, turning to Christian, "*Er-eeek-er-eeek*. You want piece of mine?" He was eating roti and pumpkin as well, but it wasn't as tantalising as Ronald's.

"No thanks, I good. Yeah, Ronald, we have a deal?" Christian extended his lunch. "Stop smiling; I serious."

Ronald bit his lip and reluctantly exchanged meals with Christian. When he removed the sandwich and skinned the white, porous bread open, a transparent slice of cheese and black shreds of air-dried mango kuchela, like black fingernail clippings, stared back at him.

"Oh *geed!*" He dropped the sandwich.

Christian stopped chomping. "Boy, how you could throw away my mother good sandwich?"

Ronald cursed when Christian rolled the foil into a tight ball and tossed it in the bin. Meanwhile, Valentin picked up the bread, cheese and kuchela and returned it to Christian's bowl.

Martin appeared. He had just finished six boxes of roti and curry.

"Ah, boy, Christian, what you eating there? Roti? Handle me piece nah."

"Look it have a sandwich there," Christian evaded, nodding at the bread, cheese and kuchela sitting on the table tennis board.

Martin smiled triumphantly. Nikita removed her thumb, but before she could say anything, he began eating, all the while smiling like a winning fool.

"Bread and kuchela," he said, gazing at the sandwich, "it strange, but it nice. It taste good, man." Martin sniffed the air. "I think George and Simone eating something in the back. See all you losers later!"

This was ten years ago. The world was different, without commitment. Today everyone is busy. From time to time there is talk about a class reunion but it almost never happens. Instead, when I run into classmates, they complain about how expensive and inconvenient these events always are, yet they fantasise and make grand plans with no substance because they recognise themselves as adults toying with adolescent ideas. So we settle for exchanging happy but lethargic memories and contradicting flavours of these old stories:

"Martin became a fireman; he still greedy like hell."

"George… you didn't hear about George? *Mama-yo!* George dead! I hear he get shoot in Afghanistan."

"Tha's a lie. George committed suicide. He hang himself with a bed sheet. His wife horn him nah. And they was only marr'ed for three months."

"Jean-Pierre going re'l good, girl. Now and then I does talk to him online. He making a lot of money. Remember how he was re'l good with computers in school? And remember how he blaze *Ugly Brigo's* ass? Lol. Now Jean-Pierre is a big boy in Silicon Valley."

"You hear Mr. Roach son get lock up for smoking weed?"

"Christian hook up with ah old thing who own a roti shop. Remember Christian? Oh gosh… he is the one who Fat Pete beat up."

"And Reinako, that provocative bitch! Imagine he settle down and does swim for Trinidad. What this place coming to?"

"I hear Ayanna and Nikita together. Humph! Well, she did like to suck she thumb."

"Mr. Ramnath was fired for impregnating a fourteen-year-old whom he married to save his ass."

"Jayden, that giggling fool! He migrated to Los Angeles for a better life and journeys on a bus six hours every day to get to work."

"G-i-r-l, you know George dead in an accident."

"Ronald lives with a common-law wife. I hear his son uses the same foil."

"Valentin! Tha' white boy had a big bottom, eh? He migrated to the cold and works as a bellhop. Imagine tha', a white bellhop."

"The one who used to make all the sound effects, Randy, he is a lawyer now."

"Stephen spends his days running his father's business into the ground. He still blazing plenty girls… and they say he have HIV."

"*Barbie*, the next Stephen, he still sucks his fingers and twirls his hair, but he get tall and strong and spends his days running a successful farm with Winston. Remember Winston? The quiet one who nobody know anything about."

"Krystal ge' pneumonia and dead. She had two lil *pickney*. Bu' she mus' be re'lly dead from AIDS. Mus' be Stephen self tha' infect she."

"Mr. Badaga and the explosive Salim Abu Muhammad still tend to the cheerless fields behind the *Agri Shed.*"

"Simone, that is the *thing* George used to deal before he get bounce down in China, pursued agriculture and works for the ministry."

"Mr. Roach is principal now. He still walks the corridors, tapping *Suzie* against his shin, his lynx's eyes missing nothing."

"The school is still there, but our class is gone."

"There can never be another like it!"

"Them days done."

"Yes, our schooldays were *the* best! Oh, how I wish I could do it all over again—"

Aye, I say, the talk going sweet eh, but I have to go and do the government work. I give the lil boy a bounce and say: wha'ever happen man, enjoy *your* schooldays.

Idle talk

Burt is most peculiar and troublesome. I had initially thought him a woman hater as on infinite occasions over lunch served in small takeaway boxes he'd blurt: "Any woman horn me they dead you know!" Spoonfuls later he'd confess, "And I not shooting anybody you know. If I have to go to jail is because I chop a man into little pieces and eat he liver." Otherwise, he was reticent. After lunch and a tall glass of mauby drink, he'd chain-smoke exactly eight cigarettes in exactly ten minutes, quick, shallow, cackling puffs that added to the heat of the dingy Chinese sweatbox where we dined everyday without fail.

Dear reader, clear your mind and consider Burt with the keenness that befits you. Now shut this book, close your eyes and meditate upon him. What do you believe is his problem? I venture to ask, would you agree that he has one? I disregarded these burning questions and only with reluctance do I admit that I learnt to ignore Burt. Instead I accepted him for who he was: a braying almost toothless imp with shifty eyes, bad hair, black lips and a cheeky mole attached to his nose. I was not starved for companionship, for on numerous occasions I had been invited to sit at the cluttered tables of co-workers and labourers who, like us, converged daily at *Tong-Fook*. But to their consternation I always stuck with Burt because his dimwitted rancour excluded him from the furtive invitations intended for me alone. In time, my practice was to hee-haw when his peculiar remarks shattered the stony silence which accompanied our meals because I interpreted them only as idle contentions. At work he was a blatant outcast and it is perhaps sympathy which prompted me to gravitate towards him.

One lazy Monday, over lunch, Burt stubbed the daily paper with his forefinger and, using his thumb, rotated it to me. He began thumping a photograph of a devious-looking fellow with a shock of white hair. "You know who that is?"

"A politician?" I glanced at Burt. "How would I know?"

"That is my father-in-law," Burt confessed.

"What!" I paused and looked at the colour photograph of Burt's father-in-law. I spat a mangled bone into my box of sweet and sour pork and noodles. "You're married?"

He nodded.

"Burt," I scoffed, "we've been working together for two years and you've never said? You don't even wear a ring."

"That's none of your business," Burt snapped. "I'm talking about my father-in-law. I killed him."

I skimmed the article. "But it says here that Mr. Roopnarine *was* bounced. It was a hit and run." The final paragraph reported that the suspect was still at large and included a police contact that eyewitnesses could call. I whispered, "Burt, was it you who bounced him?"

"No. I, my wife and he went to fish Saturday night. When we was returning home, he started to argue so I put him out the car."

"On the highway, Burt? Are you mad? So it's someone else who bounced him?"

Burt's scowl evolved into a contemplative nod accompanied by: "You think you know me. You don't. I don't take crap. My wife said I killed her father but she know to keep she mouth shut because I done tell she I will chop she up into mincemeat, and I not using a gun. And I will eat she liver!"

"What's your problem, Burt?"

"What's my problem? Nothing! I grow up poor, true, but I have a job as a travel agent now. Fifteen years ago my first wife left the country with our five-year-old son. I was the last person to find out and I haven't seen my son since. You feel I letting anybody walk over me so again?"

"Damn, damn, damn," I mumbled, still finding it weird that Burt had fathered a son and had been married: twice! "What will you do if you see your first wife again?"

"I will chop she up into mincemeat. And I not using a gun, I using a knife. And I will eat she liver!"

It struck me at that very moment that Burt was a potential murder-suicide contender and not that innocuous madman I had assumed. However, I feared not for myself but for those closest to him. I finished my meal and waited in silence as he consumed exactly eight cigarettes in exactly ten minutes. Then we left for work.

Two years later, on a bleak Tuesday, an unusually happy Burt grinned, "I doing a psychology course in the university and guess what? The professor is from Brooklyn. When he saw my surname he asked if I'm related to Benjamin. Guess who Benjamin is? My son! My professor taught my son! My surname is pretty unique, you know, so he asked if we was family. He even gave me an address in Brooklyn."

Burt was right. Frankenstein was quite an uncommon surname. "So? What does that mean?"

"How you mean what that mean?" Burt queried. "I done book my flight. I going up there, chop that woman into pieces and bring home my son." I scoffed and finished my meal. Burt smoked exactly eight cigarettes in exactly ten minutes and then we left.

I dined alone for one week.

The following Tuesday, a loud personality called me over to a crowded table in the restaurant. Waving a newspaper, the woman said, "This mad bitch is not your friend?" Burt's face was plastered across the front page. The headline read: *WANTED for murder and kidnapping. FBI joins local forces in manhunt.*

I swore. Burt's ex-wife was dead along with her husband, a federal agent. Burt's son had escaped his claws in JFK airport but Burt had managed to return to Trinidad where he eluded the local authorities. I swore again and left the restaurant but the remark, 'You and your friend is two blasted madmen,' slipped past the chimes guarding the front door.

That day, local police, accompanied by two men in dark blue FBI overcoats, descended on my workplace and seized all Burt's personal effects. They interrogated me for three hours in a claustrophobic annex we used as the kitchen. Naturally, amidst the sneers of my coworkers and familiar faces at the restaurant, I resigned from my job two weeks later, but the authorities were always able to keep track of me.

Six months later, soldiers cornered a pencil-thin Burt in Biche Forest. They tolerated him when he vowed to grind them into mincemeat, using a knife and not a gun, and eat their liver. When he actually tried they shot him. He died with a picture of his first wife and son in his cold hands. In his shirt pocket there were exactly eight cigarettes.

Relief

Martha was a mature single mother with stooped shoulders and weary eyes and she had been living in Mount Hope Hospital for eighteen months. She was a thirty-six-year-old woman with shy but pleasant features who had forgotten her beauty. Today, she was hungry, weary and unemployed. Entering an elevator, she thought, what a cheerless December. She stood to the back, staring upwards with her hands arrested. Before the elevator doors closed, she whiffed vanilla then a man entered. He wore a black suit, white tie and cologne that smelled almost edible. He wasn't particularly handsome; he was attractive. He shrugged at Martha and when she lifted three fingers, he pressed the knob for the third floor and smiled as if pleased that they were going the same place. During the ride they did not speak.

The elevator jerked to a stop. The doors opened, revealing the second floor. A nurse and two men fumbled a stretcher inside, bearing a child with white eyes and red hair, and bringing with them the smell of warm blood. Martha closed her eyes and felt herself disappear into the rear until the elevator stopped again on the third floor. The doors opened, wind gushed inside and wheels grated as the stretcher scurried away. Martha didn't hear the attractive man leave.

Outside was sunny and a dry breeze carried the scent of mowed grass but the paediatric ward with its iridescent walls and poor lighting had long shadows and a heavy silence. Martha sanitised her hands with pungent gel from the dispenser beside the sink with the large mirror. The reflection showed the attractive man wearing the black suit, white tie and smelling of vanilla, standing, talking to a nurse. Martha wiped her mouth with her hands and began walking the corridor. On one side were the waiting room, kitchen, reception desk and single occupancy wards. Nurses sat in the kitchen having lunch and speaking to each other in low tones, obscured with suppressed laughter; it was always strange to hear them laughing over lunch. Opposite, the larger wards, divided into small divisions by floor length curtains, were cramped with sick children. A woman who wasn't a nurse was pushing a trolley stacked with books. Martha waved at a mother four rooms away then peeped inside her daughter's ward: she was still asleep. At the end of the corridor she met Arlene propped against a door with her arms folded. She was stout and all expression except the one of a sad maid had abandoned her. Martha greeted her the usual way:

"How is your daughter?"

Arlene shrugged without looking up.

"And how is your son?" Martha asked. Arlene's son stayed with her on the ward. He cried himself to sleep every night.

Arlene sighed. "Okay."

"God is good," Martha said.

Arlene didn't reply. One month ago some phantom sickness had struck her daughter without mercy.

Martha sighed, leaned against the wall and folded her arms. Her stomach ached. The attractive man in the black suit, white tie and smelling of vanilla was still at the reception desk talking with the head nurse. At times he stopped and pointed towards Martha and Arlene.

"Any luck with the newspapers?" Martha said, turning towards Arlene, who barely shook her head. "Don't worry, it takes time. Everything happens in God's time."

An Indian woman with slack breasts joined Martha and Arlene. She was cradling a two-year-old boy with a surgical scar on his head. Her hair was frizzy, her eyes weary. She'd been living in the hospital with her son for thirteen months.

"Sadrani," Martha said, kissing a purple bruise on the boy's hand, "how is your son?"

"What can I say, girl?" Sadrani said, staring vacantly at her son. "What can I do?" Two weeks ago an industrial accident had crippled her husband. She and Martha spoke in low whispers until a feeble cry pulled Arlene inside her private ward.

Martha smiled. "God is good."

"How is her daughter?" Sadrani asked with a nod towards the door that had swallowed Arlene.

"Doctors still don't have a clue," Martha shrugged. "Arlene's trying to raise funds to take her to a hospital in New York but it hasn't been easy."

Sadrani asked, "How much money?"

"Seventy five."

"Thousand?"

Martha nodded.

"U.S.?"

"Mmm-hmm."

Sadrani whistled and nodded at her son: "He needs another fifteen thousand dollars for his treatment."

"God is good," Martha said.

"How is your daughter?"

"God is good." Martha stared back at Sadrani.

"And you? How are you?"

Martha hadn't anticipated the question.

"You look tired and hungry," Sadrani said. "Come let me give you something to eat before the doctors start making their rounds."

Sadrani's son's ward was in a corner next to the windows. Next to the crib was a frayed recliner–with a pink cotton blanket lapping over the headrest–and a side table with a thermos, baby bottle and bag on top. Sadrani pulled a drawer and removed a bowl with pumpkin, and roti wrapped in foil. Martha sat and while she ate Sadrani stood beside the metal crib watching her son closely as he toyed with the latch, for the rails had squeezed his hand two days ago.

"Stop it," Sadrani said to him from time-to-time.

Martha, chewing slowly, glanced around the ward. She didn't recognise a redheaded woman, a mother no doubt, sitting on a brown recliner beside a stretcher to the far end of the room, her nervous legs crossed and blank eyes glued to the floor. A man wearing a mobile headpiece stood beside her, one hand on her shoulder and the other holding the hand of the same red-haired child whom Martha recognised as the patient from the elevator. When the woman observed Martha she stood and jangled the curtains around the division. Martha turned to Sadrani, smiled and continued chewing in silence.

After eating Martha said, "Thank you, Sadrani. That was delicious." She wiped her mouth with her hands. "So when do you hope to leave the hospital?"

"When my son gets help," Sadrani replied. "And you?"

"When God wants me to," Martha stated. She burped without covering her mouth and the women chuckled. "Pardon me."

Sadrani's features tightened again. "Does your stomach still hurt from the surgery?"

Martha stood and rolled her jersey up until it was below her breasts. There was a surgical scar on her stomach where the surgeons had sliced to remove her right kidney.

Sadrani covered her mouth and exhaled forcefully. "May I?" She pressed her fingers lightly against the scar and traced the ridge. "But why does *your* daughter reject *your* kidney? She is your flesh and blood."

"God is good," was all Martha said.

A young doctor holding a clipboard against her stomach appeared on the ward. Martha and Sadrani stared as she moved among the beds, asking parents abrupt questions and jotting notes. When she approached Sadrani's son's crib and picked up a clipboard hanging from the rails, Martha excused herself, went to a window and gazed at a vulture soaring overhead. After attending to Sadrani's son the doctor approached Martha and although she didn't remember her name, she knew her daughter had less than two months to live. She consulted her clipboard and told Martha:

"I have two more patients to attend to. I'll be with you in five minutes."

"Thank you, doctor."

Sadrani had taken her son from the crib. "Doctor, excuse me, but my husband wants to know about these prosthetic legs. Are they re'lly good?"

After Martha excused herself again, Sadrani and the doctor spoke at length. Before the doctor left she told Martha, "Five minutes."

Smiling, Martha nodded then she faced Sadrani. "Good news?"

Sadrani murmured, "No, our poverty has made us prisoners."

Martha turned her attention to the world beyond the windows. The vulture had disappeared. A building away, on a second floor walkway connecting two wards, a man with a broken hand and a woman in a wheelchair were... sharing a joke. Further north was the maternity ward where she had given birth to her daughter. A hospital is really built like a prison, she thought, then remembered God. She closed her eyes and mouthed a prayer.

"Money cannot save us," Martha said, thinking of the fifteen thousand dollars her daughter still needed for a kidney transplant. Martha had raised twenty thousand through goodwill, thanks to the newspaper people whom she had put Arlene in touch with. "No, money cannot save us," she said again.

"You always say that," Sadrani said and returned her son to the crib. She tied a handkerchief around the latch, sat and pressed her head into the recliner.

Voices entered the ward. Two men appeared, waved and disappeared behind the curtains concealing the red-haired patient.

"At home I have a child who cries for my breasts," Sadrani continued, "another who is sitting S.E.A. next year, my husband can't walk. My son is trapped in here, so tell me, if this isn't a prison then what is it?" She was on the verge of tears now. Sadrani stood and Martha embraced her.

"God is good," and glancing at her wristwatch, "Forgive me but I have to go."

In the corridor Martha passed Arlene. She was speaking with the man wearing the black suit, white tie and smelling sickeningly sweet of vanilla. He was holding an envelope and although he appeared positively energised, Arlene wore that same careworn expression which sometimes made her difficult to look at.

"I'm from a non-profit organisation," he said. "A journalist you were in touch with contacted us. We want to sponsor your daughter's surgery."

Martha paused at the door to her private ward.

"Arlene," the man continued, "we're willing to cover all travel expenses and medical fees up to sixty thousand. That's U.S. dollars."

Martha pressed her forehead against the door, bent her head and gazed at Arlene: she stood on trembling knees and was sobbing into her hands. Martha exhaled, turned the cold door handle and stepped inside where her daughter lay on a hospital bed, dying and in dire need of a kidney.

Martha smiled. *God is good.*

That Internet thing

When I reach in form one my parents take a small loan and buy a computer. They get a desk with a pull out thing for the keyboard and put it in my room. I hear about some kind o' thing name the Internet, and a fellar in school hook me up with a password I didn't have to pay for. I watch porn until my back hurt, but on dial up it used to run slow, especially when is bes' quality thing y'u talking 'bout. I learn re'l tricks. I entering all kind of search string: 'Trinidad and Tobago girls,' 'Trini girls,' 'Trinidad freaks,' 'Island girls.' The list could go on but I get the best results with them keywords.

The next big thing was chatting. My whole life, I can't talk to girls in person, but man, if you see me on ICQ, asking for name, sex (as in gender) and location; anybody new log on I messaging them: *A/S/L.* I getting real hits, real responses. I lying about my age based on the woman I talking to. If them is thirty, I is thirty-three; if they is eighteen, I is twenty-one; if them is sixty-five, I is sixty-eight. You get the drift? Women always like men at least three years older because it wired into their CPU that men re'lly from Mars and that is why they so slow, because they brains doh have any oxygen.

People does say it have sick people on the Internet who does live in America, but Trinidad have some re'l freaks too. One day a girl message me; she nickname is *candilicious* and her avatar is an eye that dripping blood. This is about the same time I slow down on the cybering, so I tell she my real age. *Candilicious* was re'l cool. Tha' same day I add she to my list of special friends. When my parents think I sleeping, I in my room talking to *candilicious* because she like the same things I like, she have the same fears, she like boys my height and colour even though she never see me. Months pass and I start to fall in love with *candilicious*, but the only problem is she living quite San Fernando. We make a plan and one weekend I gone down by some family and *candilicious* and she mother pick me up. I find it strange that the mother carrying we to a pool hall to hang out. She even buying beers. Real strange, but at the same time it cool because in all the foolishness, I wishing I had a mother so. *Candilicious*, on the other hand, a little more shy than she mother. She not talking much and whenever I make a joke she saying *lol*. The mother on the other hand was more friendly. She could shoot pool good and she cracking some funny jokes – rude ones too.

On the drive back home, I sit down in the front seat. All this time *candilicious* ain't say more than a hundred words to me. I call she name and the mother answer for she, saying how she is a shy girl. Next thing I know, as we nearing we destination, moms start to talk rudeness. As boy, I tempted to answer, but as man, I say she testing me, so I play like everything she saying flying over my head. I get lil sceptical so I say don't drop me in front the house, drop me on the corner right here and call me on this number when all you reach home.

Ten minutes after I reach home the phone ring, and is not *candilicious* who calling to tell me they home but she mother. She tell me she sneaking the call and how she real like me. I cautious but the woman start to talk raw so I getting braver by the minute. I get a few confessions. The old lady tell me she is really *candilicious*, the one talking to me for the past few months and that the girl I meet is re'lly she little sister, who just went along to break the ice. In my mind I not that scared you know. I more trying to remember what the mother, I mean *candilicious*, look like. She didn't look that bad, good actually, a bit on the old side, but so what? I was accustomed to lying about my age. We talk for a good while. By the end of that conversation, we plan to meet next week. When I hang up I start to think, boy, is real sick people it have in this place call Trinidad. But I didn't let it bother me too much because, like every other man, my mentality was take it as it comes, who vex loss.

Two weeks pass and I ain't hear from *candilicious*. Anytime I log online she offline. I depressed. I miss school for a few days, hoping the call might come during the day. It never come. One day, I see a familiar face. Guess who it was? Yeah, it was *candilicious*. She face plastered across the newspapers. She did get charge for molesting a minor but she skip bail and fly out. I say, well yes, can Trinidad get any worse? Like the newspaperman read my mind: he tell me if I looking for a good time pull out the classifieds and check the *personals*; I went home with that one and log on to the Internet.

Sunday lunch

On weekdays and Saturdays, Mother cooked dhal and rice. On some days, if we were lucky, she served *bhagi* (spinach) cooked with pigtail, but the portions were always so small and so tasty, my older brothers often said that it was better they didn't get any. Mother was talented, because for years she served us the same thing and made me feel it was a different dish every day. On Mondays, she dished more rice than dhal. On Tuesdays, she flavoured the dhal with garlic, burned black and crispy in oil. On Saturdays, she swamped the rice in dhal and served it as a soup.

But on a Sunday? Ha! Food fo' so! Mother got up at four in the morning and after mass, while her sons were at the river down the hill, she and my sisters cooked their hearts out. If I close my eyes, I could see Mother, moving around the kitchen like a cat, overturning pots and pans, and chopping up seasonings gathered from the garden out back. Then, the rich Creole fragrance of baked chicken, macaroni pie, *callalou* and crab, potato salad, plantain, dasheen, white rice, watercress and stewed beef garnished with sweet peppers would envelope our home. Mmm… my stomach is growling thinking about it.

At noon, after we boys had changed, everyone stood around the table until Father came inside from attending to his bees. Boss, as we also called Father, always sat at the head of the table, his food already dished in little bowls. Mother sat opposite him. The four boys sat next to Mother, two on either side. My four sisters took up seats next to Boss.

After grace before meals, Boss would exclaim, "Fall on the enemy!"

We always ate in silence.

When everyone finished and we had placed our knives and forks next to each other in the plates, Boss would nod at each daughter, from youngest to eldest, and he'd say to Mother, "Sehr gut," and to his sons, "You all know the drill." We boys cleared the table and washed the dishes.

One Sunday, we suddenly needed room for a guest. Eric, my *big* brother, a sallow, pencil-thin fellow who hated school, brought home a bird, a doll-like Columbian named Selena, who wore way too much makeup. As the youngest, I had to give up my seat beside Mother for a stool that was higher than the chairs so, sitting behind Selena, glancing between the faces and the back of the heads around the table, I pretended I was in a cinema sitting in balcony and they were in house.

That very day, Selena dipped her fork in a dish with boiled plantain before Boss moved to give thanks. From the corner of my eyes, I saw him look up over his goggles (as my older brothers referred to his spectacles). Opposite Selena, Eric lurched forward and, to my surprise, smacked the back of her hand.

Next Sunday, Selena waited for grace, but although her English wasn't that good, she made the most of what she knew. Boss liked to eat in silence, so I knew that with each spoonful of *callalou*, he probably wanted to tell her to snap her mouth shut and eat, but he bore his burden in silence, while Mother watched him *cut eye* and rolled her pupils at Eric.

The third Sunday, Eric blurted, "Selena, shut-your-mouth-and-eat-your-food." He said it so fast that she said *si* and continued talking. Boss began eating fast. I knew he was wondering where Eric had learned to speak to ladies like that. The fourth Sunday, my eldest sister, Ava, came to the table vexed, her face squinted like a ruffled shirt. Sitting on my high stool, in balcony, I lowered my chin to my chest and glanced at Boss when she said:

"I don't know what's wrong with men nowadays! Imagine my fiancé wants to hit me because I was speaking to a man after mass."

Boss's features deepened. I knew he had lost his appetite.

Glancing between Ava and Eric, Selena said, "Hit me? *Imposible!* No man hit me! No señor!" Her eyes landed on Eric when she said, "No señor!" He stood without pushing back his chair, leaned over the food Mother had prepared and slapped Selena. Then, he left the table. Boss rocked back in his chair and froze, with his palms on the table and a bone sticking out of his mouth, staring through the front door at the gallery where Eric stood with his fists on the banister, frowning at the lawn. Mother began rubbing Selena's back. Selena began to sob.

Ava snapped, "That's good for her! She has no respect for my brother."

I jumped off my stool, went outside and told Eric, "That is not how Boss taught us to treat women."

He snapped, "What you know about woman? You lil backside!" He jogged down the steps and across the road to the river track.

Selena returned every Sunday, but Boss and Mother used to have their food in the backyard with the birds and the bees. Eric sat at the head of the table opposite Ava and because I no longer needed the stool, I sat between Selena and Ava's fiancé, in house.

Her bitter life

Perhaps you're sitting in your favourite chair reading or you're lying in bed with your legs crossed and a pillow folded beneath your head. Maybe someone is reading to you. Unless of course you're in a waiting room, you are comfortable but Seema Sahadeo's story isn't fiction, it isn't pleasant.

At birth she became the last of fifteen daughters. Her father was a bitter man who desperately wanted a son before he died. The rebel, as Mr. Sahadeo nicknamed Seema, was beaten constantly and mercilessly with blows that didn't discriminate against her anatomy. Mr. Sahadeo maintained a cold mask of masculinity when he punished Seema, developing a constable-prisoner relationship with his youngest child. Her sisters, those still unwed or, rather, unassigned to husbands of financial bonanza, though disgusted, never once dampened their father's rage. At first it was fear which kept them out but as the years wheeled by they agreed that Seema was simply too obstinate and deserved their father's wrath.

Seema learnt to comfort herself and one day, to her delight, a tractor chopped off three of Mr. Sahadeo's toes. She shook her head as her mother tended to him, disgusted by her subservience to such a pig. She noticed when he cursed from the hammock and lashed at her mother's feet with his walking stick.

After six months of bed rest, Mr. Sahadeo arranged the marriage of Seema's sixteen-year-old sister to a notorious twenty-five-year-old Casanova from Waterway. The day before the event, he tasked Seema, amused by the thought of her sister and husband-to-be smooching, with cleaning the shed. As she swept the ochre floor with a *cocoyea* broom made of dried coconut fronds she saw her father's two-toed and five-toed footprints. She giggled as a gentle wind blew gas he had released downwind.

"What you laughing at, *gyul?*" he barked.

"Nothing, Mr. Sahadeo," Seema squealed. "It just looking like a one-foot man walking with a one-foot ostrich."

She earned a severe beating and a broken hand for her mouth. The following day as she wagged her head to the rhythm of the *tassa*, she vowed that she would rather die than wed an East Indian man.

Here the story gets complicated.

Four miles east of Indianville is Accra. The two villages are quite the opposite of each other. Indianville is a strip with a mixture of mud, wooden and concrete houses decorating its borders. Accra on the other hand is where the dapper black folks live in incomplete redbrick houses.

Mr. Charles was one of these dapper folks, a man popular for being well-attired, unimaginative and very black. And he walked with a cane. While it may appear absolutely peculiar to describe him using disparate terms such as *well-attired* and *un-imaginative*, in this peculiar gentleman's case it is compulsory.

On the birth of his first son an acquaintance said, "Mr. Charles, look at you! You're a daddy now!" and, administering a firm, congratulatory shake, "What do you plan to call the young fellow?"

Mr. Charles, massaging the back of his neck with one hand and presenting a cigar with the other, said, "I'm not sure. What do you think is a good name, a strong name? Maybe David or, better yet, Goliath?"

"It's your son not mine," his friend said, frowning skeptically, "but how about Ryan?"

"That is an Indian name!" Mr. Charles hissed. "You know how I feel about those people! Heck! I wouldn't even feed my dog a roti much less name my firstborn Ryan."

"What about Charles?"

The father smiled and tapped the floor with his cane. "Not bad at all. It has a nice ring to it. Good name for a future barber. It would be something like Charles the first and second. Splendid!"

So he named his son *Charles Charles*. Charles Charles was as black as midnight. Before he turned two a neighbour donned him *Charles Chocolate*. A victim of constant ridicule, Charles Charles retracted from even his father's severe ideology and as the cold irony of fate would have it, he became a lover of East Indian food, women and culture; he adopted Conan, the barbaric adventurer, as a role model. These idiosyncrasies he kept secret, a dreadful burden which distracted and decayed his intellect. When he was sixteen, a hard-pressed Charles Senior took him out of school and employed him at the family's barber salon. Young Charles hated the work. He also despised the work of a mechanist, and after two years of loathsome toiling, he had saved enough money to purchase a car which would forever bring him heartache, stealing from him money which he earned as a taxi driver along the East West Corridor.

The car had stalled in front a hospital. Charles slammed the bonnet shut and tumbled the engine again. He pleaded but Crum did not respond so he damned the lifeless idol and returned to the carburettor.

"How far you going?"

Charles looked past his black greasy arms, propping up the bonnet. The voice belonged to a bony East Indian girl with a cleft chin and split lip. Her left hand was wrapped in a cast.

"Accra," Charles said. "You?"

"Good, I going Indianville!" Seema hopped into the car.

Back inside the car, Charles Charles said, "Listen, no disrespect, but are you allowed to travel with African drivers?" The groaning engine drowned her response as the car roared to life. "I asked you a question. You know how all you Indian from Indianville kind o' funny."

She glared at Charles and motioned at him with her broken hand.

"What happened to your hand?"

"Boy, *steups*, drive your damn car *nah*. What you want to know my business for?"

"But what the hell is this!" Charles exclaimed. "You sit down in *my* car and telling *me* to drive? No wonder my father don't like all you kind of people."

Seema tilted her head and lifted an eyebrow. "Wha' tha' supposed to mean?" Charles bit his tongue and began nursing the accelerator. While the car crawled eastwardly, he shifted his glances between his passenger and the road. After a long silence, Seema admitted, "I break my hand."

Charles sped up to a traffic light, missed the amber and stopped. "How?"

She retreated again to silence. When she looked at Charles, he was smiling thinly past pearl white teeth.

"You real *flicking* black, boy," she said casually.

The driver's smile broadened. "Yeah? I don't like it, but people call me Charles Chocolate. What is your name?"

She laughed and told him.

"Seema is a nice name. My name is Charles."

The light turned green and Charles deliberately passed a flagging passenger.

"Why you didn't stop for the old man?"

"I enjoying your company," Charles offered, surprising himself at the admission. He made a feeble attempt to withdraw the compliment.

"You enjoying my company?" Seema wanted to hear him say it again, but Charles didn't return her gaze; the road was too busy or, perhaps, so he pretended. She looked through her window. "Nobody ever tell me that."

"Me either," Charles fished.

She looked at him. "Well, I am enjoying your company too."

They looked at each other. Seema grinned. Charles smiled. Their only other conversation was based on the premise to meet again, as frequently as possible. Charles dropped Seema on Indianville junction. (Black taxi drivers never ventured into the village; no perhaps about that.) She hesitated in getting out of the car.

"Thanks for not picking up the old man," Seema said.

Charles smiled then gazed as she walked away. Before Seema disappeared, she turned around and waved.

They'd meet again tomorrow.

One year later, after a midweek escapade, Seema reached home from sewing lessons two hours past her three o'clock curfew. There were guests in the living room, four in all (two young men and an old couple), neatly arranged on the living room furniture set which was tightly wrapped in plastic that squeaked with the smallest shift. On the centre table there was a heart-shaped glass platter with grapes, dates, cheese sticks and pink strawberry wafers. Her mother was serving pear-flavoured soft drink in ice-filled glasses resting on multi-coloured coasters. Mr. Sahadeo was standing.

"Girl, sit down!" he barked and when Seema sat on a low stool, a pretentious smile crossed his face. "So, yes, um, Mr. Sookoo, this is Seema. She's a very nice child."

Seema studied the guests. Mr. Sookoo was heavyset with black, bushy eyebrows. An awkward young man with bushy eyebrows sat between him and the frail woman in a white sari. The fourth guest was a quiet young man who looked like he had bad intentions. Rubbing his stubby hands, Mr. Sookoo turned to the awkward young man.

"Ryan?"

Ryan shrugged. He was thinking about gambling. "Wha'ever yes."

Turning to Mr. Sahadeo, Mr. Sookoo apologised for his son and went on to speak highly of him and his friend, Sauna, the lovely quiet young man, whose brother was a teacher and sister was a nurse – not to mention that he had a string of *lawyer friend* and *doctor friend*. In closing, Mr. Sookoo said, "Ryan would make the perfect husband."

Seema shot up from the stool. "Wait! What you trying to do? Arrange a wedding? I not ready to marry! I is only fifteen years old! You must be feel I is one of your goat or cow."

Mr. Sahadeo snapped, "Girl, shut your mouth and sit down." For good measure he added, "Or else!"

Mrs. Sahadeo sniffled, but coughed when her husband glared.

Seema shouted: "I is not no *flicking* piece of property that you could just give away." Then she fled the room.

"Don't worry," Mr. Sahadeo said, twirling his walking stick, "she have to come back. Ryan?"

"Wha'ever yes," Ryan shrugged again. The sudden thought of his cancer-riddled mother, old and anxious for grandchildren, caused him to bob his head feebly.

Later that night, after the details had been ironed out and the guests had departed, Seema returned home. After a sound beating with Mr. Sahadeo's walking stick, she retired to bed, convinced that the matter had died.

One month later, given the depreciating circumstances of Mrs. Sookoo, hasty arrangements transpired and upon learning of them, Seema ran without stopping to her family in Peas Tree, three miles to the west.

"Uncle Boodram, hide me!" she cried. "Hide me!" Boodram promised to hide her. He locked her in the cattle shed and left on bicycle to summon Mr. Sahadeo.

The next day, Seema was unhappily married according to Hindu rites and shipped off to Quarrie, a far, unfamiliar land hidden deep in the south. The Sookoo residence was poor, but immaculate, with wooden floors and walls and curtains for doors. The two bedrooms were painted pink and the kitchen bright yellow. That night, in a dimly lit, unceremonious room, Ryan took her virginity. After he had put on his clothes and left for the casino with Sauna, Mr. Sookoo came in the room and raped her. Seema's nightmare ended in bloody sheets.

The following morning, under the re-energised bony hands of Mrs. Sookoo, Seema began her training. She learnt how to knead dough, how to clean thoroughly and how to scrub blood off bed sheets. She learned how to sew, *properly*. Mrs. Sookoo scolded her when she failed to conjure pumpkin into the sappy, smooth texture which Ryan loved.

The family Seema served was a strident lot. Soon she became their fulltime dishwasher, janitress, yard girl, sweeper, maid, cleaner and seamstress. They'd all eat while Seema served cold water and Banana Solo, and after she had cleared the dishes, the barebacked men would sit around the table, picking and sucking their teeth, disparaging her service and burping and farting as if in competition.

One night, just after Mr. Sookoo had satisfied himself and left for bed, Ryan stumbled into the room. A silhouette was behind him.

"Who the *flick* is that with you?" Seema shaded her eyes. "Charles?" she mumbled.

"Girl, just shut up!" Ryan said, hustling her onto her feet. "I loss a bet."

"What that have to do with me?"

"You is payment." He slapped Seema. "Take off your clothes!"

To his disbelief, she struck him on his nose.

"You is a man-woman or what?" he screamed and slapped her again.

She slapped him back.

They took turns slapping each other, until, finally, Ryan cuffed her unconscious, and Sauna, the winner, collected his ephemeral payment two minutes later.

The following evening, when Seema had *recovered*, Ryan confronted her. "Who you love more? Me; or Sauna?"

Seema stared at him, but didn't answer.

"What about the sex? Who better? Me; or Sauna?"

Seema rolled her eyes and looked away.

"*Ent* is me?" Ryan asked.

Suddenly, Seema thought about Charles and smiled, but, naturally, Ryan misinterpreted her reaction, so he called his parents inside the room and while they held her down, he beat her with a belt, but she only stopped cussing when Mr. Sookoo broke her left hand. That night, Mrs. Sookoo taught her how to make a splint and a sling.

From that day forth, Ryan's gambling addiction, a colourful habit incongruous with the black and white of marriage, increased along with Sauna's short-lived pleasures. He beat Seema daily, but, strange as it may seem, suicide or absconding never crossed her mind, perhaps, because her self esteem was deflated. She was trapped in a foreign land where she knew no one. Fleeing would be only a transient solution leading to further destitution. She did, however, fantasise of a better life.

One day, years later, Charles Charles was hired to do a private job that took him through Quarrie, and at one corner, when he slowed to let a stray dog cross, he saw Seema. He recognised her bony figure immediately, but didn't stop the car—he couldn't; not with four passengers in his taxi. For a moment their eyes met, and the argument she was having with two men in the well-swept yard paused. Then the men turned and glimpsed Charles.

When the car disappeared Ryan slapped Seema. "Is black man you like now?"

"I wasn't watching anyone," Seema said; perhaps she wasn't as fiery as she used to be.

"Well that was just in case," Mr. Sookoo added.

"So, you saying you feel you pregnant?" Ryan queried. "After all this time you pregnant?"

Mr. Sookoo did some calculations. The *thing* couldn't be his; she hadn't slept with him for awhile.

While the men argued, Seema's thoughts strayed to the taxi driver she had just glimpsed. It couldn't have been Charles, she thought. But what if it was? Never mind that; Ryan dragged her inside and slapped her around for sleeping with Sauna.

It would have been easier for Charles to return home via the East Coast but hoping for another glimpse of Seema, he returned along the route which snaked through Quarrie. As he approached the house where he had seen her, a woman dressed in traditional East Indian apparel ran into the road, flagging the vehicle with anxious vigour as if the devil were at her heels. Charles hunched over the steering wheel, peering below the visor. It was Seema.

When he stopped, Seema hopped into the car. Nostalgia struck: the rarefied heat of the black car, the acrid scent of sweat long absorbed into the brown cotton-polyester fabric seats and the stench of thick black grease on *him*.

"Charles, is you?"

"Seema?"

He had dreamt her every day. "Yes, yes, is me. Where you was all these years? Here? And what is all that chalk on your forehead about?"

"Sindoor!" Seema exclaimed. She laughed and without any forewarning began weeping into her hands.

"What sin you do?"

"Nothing fool." She laughed past tears. "It mean I marr'ed."

"Married?"

"Yes. But *flicking* drive we don't have time to talk!"

"What you mean drive?" She reached out with her crooked left hand and caressed his. How long was it? Five years? He pumped the gas pedal but the car stalled for the first time in weeks.

"Hurry," she said, "they probably looking for me already! I watching the road whole day, hoping is you, praying that you come back for me." Seema began sobbing again, but turned at a loud commotion. "Is Ryan! Look he *de-de!*"

The engine roared to life as Mr. Sookoo and Ryan, Mrs. Sookoo at their heels, burst from the front door and rushed down the dirt path leading to the road. Charles swore and the car sped off. Five tense miles later, he turned north onto the highway.

"I think they following we!" Seema lamented from the backseat. She was looking through the rear glass. "I think they in Sauna car."

Charles checked his mirror. "The silver one?"

"Yeah, yeah, tha' one self!"

"Who is Sauna?"

Seema glanced over her shoulder. Charles was looking at her in the rearview mirror. She said, casually, "One of Ryan friend I think I pregnant for."

Charles's heart sank. She was a virgin the last time he had seen her. "You sleeping with he partner too? You mean that is why you run away? To save your *own* tail?" He cursed Crum loudly.

"No fool! He uses to make me sleep with he when he los' money."

"Girl; you lie!" Charles scoffed. "*That* is nastiness!"

They drove in silence and three miles later, Seema confirmed, "Is them!"

"Shoot! And I need gas." Charles weighed his options.

"They just following we though," Seema shrugged.

"Listen," Charles said (Seema was glancing over her shoulder again, looking at him in the rearview mirror), "I'm going to have to stop and let you out."

"What? No, no, no! I can't go back by them people, Charles. I go dead."

Charles kept saying, "What to do; what to do?" He sighed. "Seema, look, it have something I have to tell you: I living with a woman common-law. We have a child. I mean things not that good but she is my woman."

Seema leaned over and smacked Charles behind his head. "You mean to say you living with a next woman? I thought you tell me you go wait on me no matter what happen?"

Charles glanced in the rearview mirror as he swerved into the fast lane; Sauna lagged behind. Charles accelerated and so did the silver car behind them. Charles sucked in a heavy load of air and stepped on the gas. His car had never gone so fast. It shook violently and complained noisily like a toy rattle.

Three towns zoomed past in minutes. Charles's eyes flicked between the road before him and the silver car following, closer now, his horn blearing cars out of the way. A flyover was swiftly approaching. At the last second, Charles, hunched over the steering wheel, swearing and popping the horn with his thumbs, veered dangerously across the path of a truck and onto the flyover. Instinctively, Sauna followed but his rear bumper nipped the truck and the silver car earned a mind of its own and flipped and somersaulted and flipped some more before securing itself in the median that separated the north and southbound lanes.

"Thank you Crum!" Charles celebrated. "The gods are with me!"

"Stop the car," Seema ordered. They were atop the flyover. She exited and held on to the rails, as passersby stopped below to verbally and physically assist the trio in the silver car. Her adrenaline ebbed and was replaced with emptiness. She felt a tremendous void she thought that nothing could fill. She had escaped but she didn't know at what cost.

Charles just sat there, hunched over the steering wheel and peering below the downturned visor.

Perhaps I belong to Ryan–I am mad, she thought. There is no future for us. "Goodbye Ryan," she whispered when a group of men extracted his unconscious frame from the wounded vehicle; and she prayed that his memory would fade like the cold touch of steel when her hands unravelled from the rail. She sat in the front seat and eventually fell asleep on Charles's shoulder as *he* drove *her* home.

Three weeks later, Charles Charles and Donkey, another taxi driver, sat in a popular pub along Accra junction, drinking and discussing women. Donkey found himself sniggering at Charles's problems.

Sipping a beastly cold beer, Charles shook his head. "And you call yourself my friend?"

"Charles Charles, the man who black like chocolate, you mean to tell me that you minding a child that is not yours; and another one on the way? Not to say is a pure Indian. Humph! You good yes. By the way, what your father had to say about you and Abigail?"

"Boy! He re'l glad I pu' she out."

"And Seema?"

"He ask me if I trying to *douglarise* Accra."

"Is true," Donkey frowned. "Imagine in a couple years it go have lil half-Indian children running around Accra naked."

Charles grinned, finished his beer and ordered another. "Brother man, I telling you, I not asking you, Indian woman is the best! Seema takes care of Abigail's son like is *she* child. That child does bathe on time, eat three square meals every-day—the full works."

"For real!" Donkey said. "You ain't getting no black wom-an to do them thing for you."

"And she industrious too," Charles continued. "She does sell *aloo* pies, and all them kind o' lil funny thing Indian people does make, to fellars who come to trim by the barber-shop; you know how black people like them thing! Boy, she is the best thing that ever happen to me."

Charles clutched a Stag which the bartender had slid his way; a bigger gulp this time. "Barman, your beers hot," he complained. "Wha's tha' one?"

"*Doh* study that *nah*," Donkey said. "Tell me 'bout the In-dian."

Charles sighed. "I just sorry things didn't work out earlier. She went through re'l hell y'u know."

"Humph!" Donkey had thin plaits that hung over his face like beaded curtains. "You *eat* it as yet?"

With his mouth to the bottle, Charles shook his head. "No. But don't worry. You *know* that no Indian could work their waist like me."

Slapping his thigh, Donkey roared with laughter, saying, "Eat ah food!" He was suddenly serious again. "Not once, boy?"

"No. She says it will take time. I could wait."

"You *eating* on the outside?"

Charles frowned and *steupsed* at the stupid question. "How else I will name man?"

"Anything serious?"

"I mean to say! I does still *beat out* Abigail on the side." Charles downed the remaining beer, his glassy eyes glued to the frothy liquid as it gurgled into his throat. He burped. "But I love Seema."

"You drinking fast, boy. You want a next one?"

"I good," Charles said, waving his palms. "I going and pull some bull there, see if I could make some money. Have to check Abigail later and then home time; eat some good Indian food." Sticking his tongue out, he massaged his belly and exited the bar.

It was almost midnight, a quiet night except for faint music from the pubs on Accra junction. The Charles residence was still. *Charles Charles* slipped the key from under the front mat and entered. He tossed his car keys and a newspaper on a chair and went to the kitchen. He smiled; there was a plate wrapped in foil on top the dinner table. He sat, murmured a memorised grace and ate *his* meal with a knife and fork. After, he burped loudly; Seema entered, cradling Abigail's son.

"Pardon me," Charles said and covered his mouth.

"Any news of them?" Seema asked.

"No baby," Charles said, flicking his collar towards his nose; there was a trace of Abigail's perfume. "No news of Ryan or Sauna. And nothing in the newspapers since the article about how Mr. Sookoo was paralyzed from his waist down. Relax. They probably gave up searching for you."

"What about my family? You learn anything?"

"Beyond your father being a one-foot diabetic with two toes, no."

"Humph. How come you reach home so late, Charles?"

"Plenty people on the road, baby."

"How much money you make today?"

"I make a hundred," Charles said but perhaps he didn't have any money in his pockets so he added, "I loan Donkey some money."

"Are you still seeing Abigail?" Seema asked and began raking her bottom lip with her teeth. She knew the truth. Charles's eyes twinkled before he answered; they always shone when he lied. How ironic, she thought. "Your clothes for tomorrow ironed and in the room," she said, changing the topic. "I'm inside whenever you ready."

"Honey," Charles stopped her, "you know I love you right?"

Seema twisted her lips into a smile but hid her teeth. She nodded and turned to leave.

"I didn't hear you, Seema." Charles's voice was assertive, commanding, but in it no guile.

"Yes baby, I know you love me. I love you too."

"Thank you for the food. It was great. Creole belly full!"

Seema chuckled and although she knew she had been appeased quite easily, she felt sadly contented. Her life was no longer one of servitude, nor was she some emissary serving the omnipotent, omniscient Deities: Ryan, the Sookoo family and Sauna. Charles Charles was good to her. He had his ways, his horrible vices but he was always affectionate, always intimate. She smiled and placed Abigail's son in the crib. In the bathroom, a bucket was filling with water. Thinking of Charles naked, pouring water over his head and body, she removed her clothes and lay in bed. She was ready.

When Charles entered the room, she took his towel and, kneeling on the bed, pressed her baby bump against his back and while drying his chest, she nibbled at his neck and ears. They made love with Charles still wet. She ignored the unfamiliar perfume on his neck. Tonight, Charles thought of Seema. Perhaps tomorrow Charles wouldn't think about Abigail. Perhaps he'd think about Seema alone–perhaps.

Alley-loo-yer

At exactly half past ten, nighttime, Half-ah-Bob walked in. Now Half might not be your ideal guest for a family-village get together because as you well know, Half tired do time behind bars for all kinda petty crime. But Icacos is a special kind of Village. When yuh down there under them sweet coconut trees, yuh really forget de rest of Trinidad exist. Everybody is *family*. And it easy to get ah fish from dem fishermen on the beach. And if yuh help them haul up the boat yuh might even get five extra fish. So when Half walk in, nobody pay him any mind. But is the way he make the grand entrance that stop all conversation. Shiny pants, shirt open down de front, nice jersey, cigarette dangling from right hand and ah empty *styrotext* cup in the next hand.

"Eh, eh, like ah in time to wake up this party," Half say. And with dat, he launch out with a series ah classical Indian tunes, old and current. The boys want to support Half but he changing tunes too fast. And the fellars coming in for a little rebuke too. "Wha' happening, fellars? Give me a little backing nah. Just a little backing with bottle and spoon and ah go show yuh real performance."

Bottle and spoon chip in. But Half moving so fast, cockroach and all afraid to cross he path.

Somebody in the lookout upstairs say, "Pass the bottle," and Half ask for excuse.

Icacos have some real cinema characters, yes: *Pickin* sitting in a corner, hair white like snow, minding she own business picking through she plate of buss-up-shut and curry chicken; *Cochee* with she face serious, serious like Apache Chief Cochise; *Archie* grimacing like Jughead because he drink too much; *Miss Cynthie*, village teacher, who want to retire bad-bad, sitting like she waiting for roll call; *Polly*, village shopkeeper, eyeing *Mills* who credit get long-long-long; *Miss Sharida*, who tight pants straining at the seam and mouth red-red like Negril sunset; *Boom*, who take all he hair off he head and wearing it below he chin; and *Frankie*, who belly so big everybody want to know when the baby go born. Look, even *Jap* here. Jap grow up in Icacos selling in *Miss Lucy* shop. Miss Lucy could hardly speak English, but so she coulda quarrel. But not Jap; he was real quiet. Now he living in Fullerton, about four miles away. But he love Icacos. Nobody know if he does miss he mother since she gone. Is twelve years Miss Lucy dead and still Jap ain't have a wife. Somebody say he doh like quarrel.

Well, Half-ah-Bob chip downstairs and get real spiritual.

Somebody whisper, "It look like Caroni spirit working on Half-ah-Bob. Watch out."

With half ah smile, he face turn half-way to the light as though he profile is the nicest thing in de world, Half-ah-Bob declared: "Brothers and sisters, this is the season of goodwill;

ah time fuh sharing and caring. So leh we offer up praise; *Alley-loo-yer*. Ah qualify to offer praise; *Alley-loo-yer*. Ah do three years in Point Fortin rehab with a church group; *Alley-loo-yer*. Yuh should see me in three-piece suit. Louise, if yuh see meh in dat suit! Girl, yuh would ah leave Lance fuh meh; *Alley-loo-yer*." Like a race-horse out de box, Half start with *Amazing Grace* followed by *When the saints go marching home*.

Meanwhile, John sitting with both feet on de table taking in de scene. Now, John is a man wid a little domestic worry, so when Half-ah-Bob transferred all his energy into *Leave your burdens down by the riverside*, John get all sentimental. Hands went up, clapping. A tear or two rolled past John's moustache. "Yeah Bob... yeah Bob, yuh know de ting."

Trouble is, Icacos don't have no river. As fast as Half started, he stopped. With great finesse, he put the Styrofoam cup on the table. Now on dis table yuh had a choice of blends: rum, whiskey, wine, beer.

"*Alley-loo-yer*," crooned Half. "John, boy, the devil fighting meh bad, bad. Come, take ah drink wid me."

But John refused: "I overs dat. De devil cah win me there."

Tantie Louise, who laughing and singing with Half, turn to she little niece, Whitney, and say: "Clear de table. We doh want Half to lose de battle wid de devil."

I didn't tell you about Colombo. He is Half bigger brother who like to tell people Half born with a veil over he eyes. "Mama say Half could see things nobody else could see."

"Ah pity he didn't see all dat jail he had to make," *Pickin* whispered, over she glass ah sorrel and ginger beer.

Well, Colombo get up nice and easy from he seat and approach the table. "Before yuh clear de alcohol, leh me tell yuh ah ain't have no quarrel with de devil. Alley-loo—" The glass was full of rum before the word 'yer' was heard.

Half rock back on his heels, tugging at invisible suspenders. "One night in Point, ah dress up sharp-sharp and gone to preach. Round meh neck was a microphone and ah small speaker. See meh at Frisco Junction. Brothers and sisters—"

"Yeah," John chimed in, "ah was passing that night and I say, buh wait-dat is Bob. Buh wah the hell—"

"*Alley-loo-yer*," Half-ah-Bob smiled. "Is me self yuh see. Ah tell dem, brothers and sisters ah have ah message from de Lord. He send meh to tell yuh to repent." Half closed his eyes as if seeing the scene right there and then. "But," he went on, "dem Creole give meh hell dat night."

"No, Bob. Come nah man, you should know better than that," cut in Wayne, grimacing as he shifted in his seat, grimacing because his back was hurting like mad! "Lower back problem," he would explain, "but ah biting the bullet. Ah bearing meh pain."

Now Wayne is a military man and how many bullets he had bitten was something Archie wanted to find out for the longest while. He wondered too, whether Wayne, who was also his coconut Estate Manager, didn't want to bite on a hand-grenade instead.

"No Bob," Wayne repeated, "we don't use that language round here. Not in my home!"

"But," Half protested, "ain't no Creole here; except Lance; and he more red than black; *Alley-loo-yer*."

At this point, Archie, like most of the other guests, drifted home. John felt Half had enough, so he held Half's hands and almost gently put him to sit. Half was pensive for a while, then bounced out of the chair.

"No, John," he said, "that was a stroke of de devil. He want meh to keep quiet. No way!"

Archie returned, his face all screwed up like a sick zaboca. "Wayne, Wayne! It have a set ah fellars by me and dey want to beat meh. Come put dem out."

"Oh gosh, Archie, I kar jus come dey and do dat. Is yuh brother house too. Is his friends too."

"No… Wayne, go an run dem."

"Then come wid me."

"Nah, you go alone."

Colombo was exasperated. "But what I hearing. Yuh want Wayne to go an you stay? That man is higher than the Police Commissioner. He is ah Lieutenant in de Navy. Suppose he go and we hear Bam! Bam! And Wayne dead on de floor. And yuh over here. What people go think?" He steupsed hard.

Meanwhile, Half-ah-Bob vex, vex. Like de devil get de better of him. He not saying ah thing; he just looking hard-hard at Archie. "Okay, I know what yuh need, Archie. Yuh need ah little praying on. I go help yuh." Half walk across to Archie and place his left hand on Archie's forehead.

Archie close he eyes as if he go receive some sort ah deliverance.

"The power above," Half began, "help this bother to find peace. Go and drive out from his house, all dem fellars. Tell dem is time to leave; *Alley-loo-yer.* Tell dem to leave Archie alone; *Alley-loo-yer.* And take Jesus out dis devil; *Alley-loo-yer.*"

How Half come up with this line, nobody know, but like a snake striking, Archie's eyes sprang open and he grab Half-ah-Bob hands. "Yuh calling me ah devil? Who is more devil than yuh!" He looked threatening.

Half turned away with pontifical contempt. "Yuh don't need spiritual help. Yuh can't get help. Look yuh better go home before ah give yuh some good hot slaps."

The party break up, but before daylight, we hear Half and Colombo had a good brotherly fight in their own yard, with John giving the parting speech.

See yuh in Icacos.

Finding myself

I have always regarded education at arm's length. Frankly I mistrust the institution. I treasure knowledge yes, but there is a hazy promise which I reject: 'Lyndon, get your education,' people would say, 'because i's only then you could get a big work with the oil industry.' This is a sham. Recruitment adverts are also shams, for they demand education and another crucial item. Have you guessed it as yet? Yes, it is *experience*. Through this mechanism they are able to suppress wages. Yet students are honed to believe that on exiting university a five digit salary *will* be hitting their bank accounts. Mind you there are honest men like Rabbit, a mechanic living opposite me, who never cared for school yet he is always armed with a coil of money. I do not suggest that success is *business success* but alas it is the way of the world. The neighbour behind me, Mark, is a bigwig by society's standings, honoured with a first class degree from a university in New York, and he doesn't even own a car – and he is a loans officer. Yet people urge me to be like him rather than Rabbit.

The day after my last Caribbean Exams Council (CXC) exam, I told my parents, "I'm never going to school again."

They were sitting in the gallery. My father said, "Good idea!"

"Yes," my mother added, "our finances are a bit tight. Don't worry I'll get you a job so you can contribute to the home."

I was dumbstruck that they had so readily agreed. The following Monday I was dressed for work: starched shirt, pants, tie and slicked shoes. I arrived late and the uncompromising, unforgiving, flint-faced manager dictated my portfolio. My job as a courier was pretty straightforward; I waited for a wire platter to fill with envelopes (or one urgent item) then delivered them to the marked addresses.

Maybe you're familiar with Port of Spain: the skyscrapers under construction, the narrow, dirty streets and drains, the vagrants you cross the road to avoid, the irritable drivers, the waves of solemn pedestrians. For the greater part of the day I walked around the capital with my tie slackened, sleeves rolled up and jockey shorts wet.

One day, as I stepped off a pavement, a taxi knocked me flat on my back. As I tumbled across the road and into a drain, the driver cursed and sped off. One block down, having barely recovered, I encountered two police officers. I cocked my elbow, showing the gravel on my arm.

"Officers, I have a report to make! Ah taxi now bounce me down! The car number is HAO 6–"

"Wait-wait-wait-wait-wait!" the taller officer interrupted. "You need to make that complaint by traffic branch."

"But all you right here," I argued, "and the man bounce me down, cuss me and drive off."

"What he tell you?" the other officer asked.

"He cuss me."

"What he say?"

"Repeat it as it happened?" I asked, squinting.

They both nodded.

"He say: '*Coolie*, get your f-ing tail out of the road!'"

The taller officer reached for his baton.

"Young fellar," the other warned, "you want to get lock up this hour o' the morning for cussing breeze?"

I stared at them in disbelief and went about my duties.

That Friday I was paid $235.41 – broken down by the old, rusty-haired cashier into two blue notes, a purple twenty, one grey ten, a green five; the forty-one cents came in coins, strangely, one of each that Trinidad carries. On paper, and with an almost nine percent increase in inflation since then, this figure would appear quite small and, indeed, it is. In American dollars it's $37.36 which meant that per day I made USD $5.33. (At the time I was not saddened by the fact that more than 1.8 billion people live on less than USD $2.00 per day.) I was rich! It was unthinkable that at seventeen I had managed to escape the financial wings of my parents who had fed and clothed me for a lifetime [and would continue to]. I was like a chick that had outgrown the mother hen.

Months passed. I was a good courier but my pay began to look small as my vices increased. I had picked up smoking and drinking. Instead of taking sandwiches to work I purchased lunch. I no longer helped at home. When money was low, I requested cash for travelling expenses and opted to walk to my destinations. When my conscience prevailed I went hungry.

I had altogether forgotten about school when CXC results came out. My results weren't as bad as I had expected. I had obtained a full certificate with so-so passes in English, Biology, Mathematics and Agriculture, a double award subject.

My parents said, "Good job, Lyndon."

But I knew that if measured against prestigious standards I was a failure. How peculiar. Back then I believed that my parents were more naïve than informed but despite their honesty, times had changed; I was not *crème de la crème*.

In time my work portfolio was decorated with more "professional" responsibilities but my salary never budged. Three months later I was still conducting CSR duties and being paid as a courier. I was unhappy with this lack of recognition but I said nothing to my employers. I opted to leave the job. Within two weeks I was unemployed and under the financial wings of my parents who had grown accustomed to my *freedom*.

"Guess what!" my mother shocked me one afternoon. "You got a pay raise!" She had been involved in secret negotiations with my ex-employers.

I was back on the job. I would be paid monthly through the bank but I didn't have an account and I procrastinated in setting one up so at the end of the first month I collected a cheque. I remember being paged to the director's office. He was sitting in a leather-bound chair behind a desk swamped with documents. The accountant was standing behind him with her hand on the backrest. She slid a cheque from a folder, passed it to him and she and I watched as he slowly extracted a fat golden pen from his pocket, fastened the cheque to the desk with his forefinger and scrawled his signature as if he despised it. The manager took the cheque, stapled it to my payslip, folded and sealed the items in an envelope which she stapled and passed to me reluctantly as if it were her money. I backed out of the office and hurried to the toilet.

You wouldn't believe my excitement, the waves in my stomach as I sat on the toilet cover and prised open the envelope. I closed my eyes; I inhaled deeply; I opened my eyes; I exhaled; $2773.37! My goodness! From $235.41 a week to *this* figure was singularly incomprehensible. Ha! I wish I had photocopied that cheque.

Like a pay cheque, a lot of people are nice but only on the surface. When I was courier I thought the staff was a jolly bunch because I was outside for the most part but now, working among them, I wasn't so sure. After two months I was tired of their complaining. 'Don't trust those ladies,' one man frequently confided, 'they are the bacchanal section; always in other people business.' 'Stay far from the Indians,' advised another, 'because they like to brown nose with the boss.' 'The Africans,' a supervisor once told me, 'they lazy like hell. I could be getting paid to do all o' them work.' How disturbing and shameful! If you're a senior employee let me tell you that it's distressing for a newcomer, more so a teenager, to work among fretful men and women. Don't seek out these rookies to form shaky office coalitions which are arbitrarily broken.

I worked with an exception to this irksome *rule*, a big-nosed Englishman who showed me the ropes. He came to work at eight o'clock, worked nonstop, except for an hour lunch, and left at four-thirty sharp. One Thursday, to everyone's surprise, he and I worked late into the evening because of a deadline. After, he invited me to play snooker at an old-timers club he belonged to.

"This game," he said while he lined up a shot with the black ball, "in no way suggests that we are friends. On the job we are co-workers, nothing more, nothing less." And he was true to his word. At work we talked only if we required help. What's wrong with that? We weren't there to make friends—we were there to make a living.

A client I knew only from speaking to over the telephone walked into the office one day, a beautiful Chinese girl, leggy, unusually tall, with straight, black hair that touched her butt. After I attended to her, we chatted about school.

"What you going and study in America?"

"Like, I'm going to do, like, psychology," she piped.

Squinting and nodding, I crossed my legs and clasped my knee with both hands.

"You'd, like, so totally love it!" she exclaimed.

That evening I told my parents, "I'm going to do psychology!" They must have groaned at, "And, like, I'm leaving my job."

One month later, I enrolled at the university. The first semester included: English, Sociology and Organisational Behaviour. Educators, it is perplexing when a student registers for a discipline only to discover that there would be nothing but foundation courses in the first semester. Please, mix and match! Please.

Two months later, the Englishman and I were playing snooker on Thursdays, since my game had improved upon returning to my *stationary* post. School was a ghost. Additionally, the discontentment at the office had grown. One woman continually groaned like a weary cow. Would I grow old and trapped like her? Or would I be like the man whose bar tab surpassed his salary every month? Maybe, I thought, I would be like that mother who came to work late every morning because she had three kids to drop at three different schools, and constantly faced the manager's wrath. Flustered by these thoughts, my job suddenly sickened me.

At the time my brother had just resigned his job. Newly-wed and with one kid, he needed money badly. We decided to rear poultry, an idea which, today, no one owns up to. At that time ducks fetched a whooping fifteen dollars per pound. Our collective savings became capital. Finally, I had a good reason to leave my job. One week later I went to the direc-tor's office.

I said, "Boss, I'm leaving the job."

He was about to sign a cheque but stopped. "Why?" The accountant stood behind him, smiling.

"To mind ducks."

He laughed. "Wait. You're serious? You're leaving selling stationery to mind ducks? You thought about this seriously? Think about it and let me know."

The next day, I was at my brother's helping him put down a foundation. He did most of the work, using bamboo, bind-ing wire and galvanise sheets to build a fifteen-by-fifteen pen. After, we drove around Trinidad in my parents' car, purchas-ing livestock. Within weeks, the yellow ducklings began to mature into white ducks. Profits loomed in the air. While he worked and I rested, he'd say:

"Lyndon, sixty ducks, each weighing nine pounds and at fifteen dollars a pound, you know how much money that is?" After a tedious day, he'd point north and fantasise, "All them

Indian going Caura River love duck. People will buy, man, people will buy."

Independence Day we heard screams. When we rushed outside, a dog had killed every single duck. The greedy bitch had not eaten one; it was simply wanton destruction. My brother cried that day; it was natural: we had just lost $8,100.00. He spent the next two days hunting the dog and eventually shot it with a homemade crossbow. I often wonder if it is this incident which nurtured his underlying distaste for man's best friend.

We adapted. We built a pen the size of a small yard. I can't recall how but we bought an additional one hundred and sixty ducks. We fed them anything: from pellets to fish guts. They grew nicely, although nowhere as extraordinary as the first batch. Then, one day, they simply began dying. We'd go to the pen and there would be two or three ducks lying in a dehydrated daze as if struck by paralysis. They died until only their ashes remained. My brother eventually got a job which he still has.

So much for ducks; I was back at the stationery store! Under new management they had computerised the business. Perhaps because of my exposure I wanted a desktop. My parents loaned me money and I purchased a Dell Dimension L100 which was promptly shipped to my work address. That afternoon is engraved in my memory. At four-thirty, my brother picked me up in a car he had purchased (with earnings from his new job) and I loaded the vehicle.

That evening, I struggled together the colour-coded computer peripherals. I learnt about software. I mastered creating, reading, updating and deleting files. I learnt about the Internet and email. I learnt about computer programming. I purposed: I must know how this works. I convinced my mother that her credit card was safe online and purchased a text on C++ which I couldn't comprehend beyond the preface. Suddenly, I *wanted* to go to school to learn. Most people believe that they *need* to go to school to succeed, to leave dead-end jobs, particularly CSRs.

Like other parents, mine must have been anxious about my indecisiveness. If you're a parent it's natural to want the best education for your child but don't assume that what you think is best *is the best*. Am I saying to let your children determine their own future? Yes. Sure you can advise them but remember you're a parent, not a dictator. Right now you're scratching your head and saying that's tough because, using the division of labour as a guide, you may assess your child's passion as having low monetary returns. So what? Before you spend thousands on tertiary education, send your child out to work. Let them sell limes at the street corner, cut lawns in your neighbourhood or work in a Syrian cloth store. These aren't preposterous ideas. At sixteen, most teenagers have already smoked, drank alcohol or have sex. But they don't know about work. All too often I consult with young students who wish they were doing something else, perhaps, nothing at all. But they're sticking it out, losing money, grumbling about it, insomuch that completing their degree is like watching a stupid movie past the first hour. Teenagers who get a job straight out of secondary school have a better chance of later educating themselves in a field they really care about rather than those who go through a course set by themselves or their parents. Create avenues for your child to explore. There's more harm in not experimenting, pretty much like it's risky to believe that God doesn't exist.

Now let's talk to the youth. The world is large and possibilities are endless. Never doubt yourself and feel free to dream. We are happiest when we do what we love and we are most successful when these actions are within the law that guides our faith. Do not reject advice for your parents or guardians were once young. Often times the path to our dreams is through their wisdom. Say your parents want you to be a lawyer but you want to play for the West Indies cricket team. If you really love cricket what's to stop you from pursuing it in your *spare time*? There's no harm in having multiple goals. Remember, knowledge is power; education empowers. I know this, even though at times I am a stubborn fool.

Man on a mission

It was Saturday morning and my partner Thomas was with me. I'm John, a muscular fellow. I could prove it: a girl once mistook me for The Incredible Hulk. The problem was I wasn't green so she made me out. Thomas and I are great friends. When I want to do something crazy, he does put some sense in my head and when Thomas gets in trouble with those gangsters, that's where I come in! Let me tell you though: I'm always prepared with a hundred-yard rope that can expand and contract. Anyway, Thomas and I are going to the cinema tonight to watch a show with some spacemen going to space.

Later that night, Thomas and I went our separate ways and headed to our houses. I dreamt about that show and swore I was drooling because somebody started beating me with a beam – a moonbeam – and when two pitching stars laughed at me, I flexed my muscles and they disappeared.

In the morning, around ten, Thomas and I met and I started talking with my big, blabbering mouth. I say I want to go up in space! Well let me tell you this: for sure Thomas not changing my mind this time!

I head home, pack some food, get some attitude from my next-door girlfriend and head to NASA. I paid a man some money to go to the moon with one of those high-tech suits. I was sure that my girlfriend dumped me because she like a psychic and she know that I going to die or so at least she thinks. But, whatever, I going to stay on the moon for six days and I think it will be an enjoyable time. I quickly got in the rocket, the man start the engine and off we went!

Meanwhile, inside the rocket, my belly start to hurt me since it's a five-hour trip! Well, boy, I pull out my bag and start to eat like mad! When I finished I start to walk around. Now, I don't know where everything is, but I was looking at the labels on the doors to see which room is which. Curious, I saw a door with no label and was tempted to go inside there. I turned the rusty doorknob, my heart pounding as quick as a horse in a story called *Chasing Sevens*. When I look in that room, I fall down meters away from the rocket fire, saved by some handlebars hanging nearby. I shouted for help. As I said I do indeed have a blabbering mouth. Of course one of the astronauts heard me and sent a rope for me to come back up.

Finally the time had come, indeed I was truly *ex-tatic*! I set my first step on the grey, dusty particles, watching around in amazement, and fully armoured in my suit, I bounced around and explored. By the time I reached back to where the rocket had landed it was gone!

Well, boy! I wanted to wet my pants, because killing myself wasn't an option, as I didn't have a knife. I started walking around and decided to eat something. Quickly, common-sense prevailed as I realised I forgot the bag with everything inside that wretched rocket. Well, I thought I was doomed, but I remembered and said to myself:

"John, who are you boy? You are the expanding Robocop, you deal with them gangsters!"

I got back to my old self and set up a fight for survival. I walked around like John Rambo and started to see what I could get to eat. Then I remembered a trick my dad taught me: if you want to eat and there's no animals or any food, what it was you had to do was tear pieces of your clothes, warm up your hands by rubbing them together and place them on the rolled up clothing; what the heat does is that it softens the clothes which makes it easier to eat through. Of course anybody would know what to drink: it would be saliva or urine.

I felt like I was eating cotton on an average scale of good and bad, and the saliva is an everyday thing, but I wasn't so sure about my urine though. So when that was done, I went in a cave and sheltered for the night. Pretty much that was how my five days went. Then I realised I have to get the hell out of here before I end up eating my aluminium air tank.

I remembered I had my one-hundred yard rope. I must mention I'm great with both a lasso and technology. So I tied a loop on one side and lassoed it to a satellite. I took a medium-sized boulder and placed it on top of the other end of the rope. Luckily, I got some wisdom in rope climbing from the rocket incident five days ago.

I climbed on the satellite and connected with the NASA company. I told them I was stranded on the moon and to come to pick me up. We ended our conversation by NASA asking how did I connect with them and I responded I was on the satellite and I still had a layer of clothes as I had worn normal clothes underneath. I had eaten everything except my helmet and air tank. At last the time came when another rocket arrived. On the way to earth I fell asleep.

When I woke up NASA debriefed me and I went home. I was right: my girlfriend had dumped me. But I was more vex with the man who left me on the moon. When I remembered him, three words went through my mind: *the hunt begins.*

The teenage man

I recoil, exposing a cheek which falls victim to her coarse palm. I've been humiliated in front victims and bullies alike. The world becomes smaller and I stand out the most, a boy humiliated by a girl, of all people. I could feel her hands in my pockets even as she walks away a few dollars richer. She certainly knew about perseverance and she most definitely knew about success. I could do the same I assure myself as I correct my posture and chew my mouth to ease pain and feign toughness. I would persevere and succeed, I would survive. I would become tough by going without lunch and walking home from school. Without money I had no choice. In one year, I would grow. I consoled myself. Yes, a year would result in two things: a bigger, stronger me and the climb from form one to two.

I've grown a bit. I seem to be heavier in fat than in actual muscle, however, there are people smaller than me now. The form ones this term seem to have shrunk a bit. Acne explodes on my face and for a few months I am the target of constant ridicule. I still walk home and it gives me the opportunity to pass two college boys on their way home as well. I've heard them sneering at me. One even dared to look at me for a few seconds. For the first time in my life I felt what it was like to rock a slap on somebody. The excitement and rush literally snaked its way up my neck. They really think they are better than me don't they? Given the chance I would make every school in the country equal just to take that joy from them. Let them see where brains can get them when every school is at a junior secondary level. They would have to learn to survive. They would have to grow up into a man, just like me.

Form three isn't that bad. The new students are even smaller than the previous year, or maybe it's just the fact that I am a bigger man. Can you imagine that I have become a man even before I have left school? What would I become when I leave this place? I now have enough rank to keep my money and make a few extra *reds* on the side. I am safe. Some of the boys even trust me enough, so I have gotten an insight into what a dirty magazine looks like past the cover. It feels wrong at first, but then I get these strange feelings that I instantly recognise as something addictive. I'm a bit confused by the secrecy my friends place in this magazine; however it's not wise to ask questions. Maybe it was wrong, but then how can something so great be wrong? If it's wrong I can't ask my father, my teacher or any adult about it. Can I? I can't. They are too busy either way, focusing on something bigger than me, something that does not relate to me, something I can't be part of. I guess I would just have to shut up and learn from my friends. We do have each other after all. I could live here forever. I've grown to love this place.

When it seems that I have just made my name, I've been picked up and thrown into something I can only describe as hell. After suffering the painful separation from the school I love they ask me to choose subjects for CXC. They tell me that these subjects I choose would determine what I want to be in the future. That's funny. I don't even know what I want to be. I know I am a man, but that is as far as it goes. How can I know more when I don't know what it's like? I have fantasised about becoming a policeman, but maybe, if a real policeman spoke to me I would know what it was really like. I consult my parents, but they mutter something about being a man. At least they know that much. Physical Education and Art should be easy subjects to pass. I have made my choice and the only thing left to be done is to fit in with the cool guys and climb further up the food chain.

I bash myself for initially hating this place. I've grown so much. The guys here are a lot cooler. Cigarettes and marijuana, which once made my chest scream, now glaze the lining of my throat and bask my lungs with its sweet intoxication. I can clean marijuana like a professional: I can roll it in bamboo paper and lick it sufficiently enough for it to stick, but not ruin the paper. In the year 2005 I would be known as a *ganja farmer*. The funny thing is that the police, the teachers and the parents can't stop us. They don't even look at us, right? So how can they see what's wrong? It has struck me as odd that they don't realise the same criminals they are dealing with were most likely moulded in secondary school. Someone should tell the fools.

I'm on fire. My mind is burning and so is my territory. It's amazing how tough and big new students are. My form five brethren was stabbed with a compass, while taxing a little punk. The teachers watched him die. My friend probably could have been saved, but they didn't want to get involved – as always. Someone must help us! Someone must do something about this mad society! How can the mad help the mad? I would be happy to leave this place, go out into the real world and start over. Show them the man I have become in my teenage years.

I'm proud on the day I receive my examination results. My grades are certainly not that bad for a guy who never went to class. I'm elated, only to have my hopes smashed by my parents who suddenly have time to talk to me. I learnt that it wasn't nine ones I had, but a III in Art, a III in Physical Education and a III in English Language. What can I do with that? Suddenly, I am scared. Suddenly, I realise that I probably ain't man enough. I would have to do something about that.

With grades like this I have learnt that I can qualify as an officer of the law. I would teach anyone who wants to be a bigger punk. Isn't that hypocrisy? How can I become an officer of the law when I have done and continue to do all these things that are deemed inappropriate by society?

Maybe I could use my new position to change policies. Maybe I could legalise marijuana. Surely they would see things my way – they always have. I could use my position to do so many things. Regardless of what I do for work, there are so many ideals that must be shared. If everyone that came out of school within the next ten years was like me then society would be a different place. It would be normal to do what is considered wrong today. It all depends on the students of the future to finish what I have started. I fear that people who can make positive changes may recognise where the problem lies. This, though, is unlikely. I can only pray. In the meantime, I would shake down the college boys who sneered. I would keep the unknown cycle which society is trapped in alive. Like me, youngsters can learn from each other and not depend on adults to share their experiences.

I now have a bigger school to play in; society is, after all, a big unruly school, and I am its principal. Only now do I possess the power to further prove my point. I can now be a man, a teenage man.

Tabby

Tabby's frown pleated his forehead. His lips formed a small smile as he felt the cutlass's edge with his thumb. Its razor sharpness brought him great satisfaction. He placed the file away and concealed the weapon in another location. Through a crack in the pitch pine board he watched his wife as she texted someone whom he felt sure was her lover. He cursed himself, hating the insecure person he had rapidly become.

"Imagine I spying on my wife," he muttered, stepping back from the musty board.

Countless times, for the past month or so, he confronted her with his suspicions. It was only until now he had come to the realisation that his precious wife was a big liar. He cursed at technology as he heard the symphonic ring of her phone. Even the poor man could afford this new-age device that had become dog cheap, a device that was instrumental in deteriorating his relationship with his *love*.

He walked over to the latrine which stood alone, tall overgrown grass brushing against its galvanised walls. His magnificent yard now resembled the many surrounding homes.

Depressed at that thought, he sat on the wooden seat, pondering his life's achievements: a home, a fridge, a television and a bed. His old BMX bike leaned against a shed that adjoined the house. A water tank collected the rain. He shook his head. It used to seem like so much, now he saw his true poverty. A wagging Sally poked her head through the half opened door. He patted her and softly whispered:

"Good, girl, you're a good girl."

Tears broke out and he stifled his painful moans.

That afternoon, Tabby called for a drink of white rum as he pulled a wooden stool closer to the bar counter. After diluting the drink with cold water he quickly gulped it down. He shook his head, disgusted by its taste. His drink was beer by choice, but it took too long to drown his worries so he had moved up the ladder for a stronger drink, a drink that would numb his tired mind. He ordered another half and moved away from the other cheerful drinkers to a table that stood alone in a dark corner. Fixing himself another drink, Tabby lit a cigarette. He thought about her.

"How could she do this to me?" he whispered. "She shows me no respect." Imagine leaving the house offering no explanation, he thought. I don't even know if she gone by a friend or to a party. If I ask her she telling me when I go to drink she don't ask me where I was. But at least she knows where I is! Tabby steupsed and took a sip of rum. The alcohol eased his brains. He placed his index finger into a pool of water surrounding the bowl of ice. He dragged the finger aimlessly, leaving trails of lines and circles. His hurt was deep, his thoughts were overwhelming. He knew he should just let her go but couldn't. He knew that the man she was involved with was not responsible yet he blamed him. He wanted revenge. But on whom? The man was *getting* from his wife. Why shouldn't he take?

"No! He have to dead for that, boy!" Rum cut in. "That man all over your wife. Boy, kill he! Drink and we go fix he tail with that sharp-no-arse cutlass you have home!"

Night had fallen and Tabby sat on his bike's saddle. He pedalled quickly hoping momentum would prevent him from falling.

"I have to get my cutlass! He is a dead man tonight, then I go see about she, then me!" He felt crazy. "Blasted lights!"

Tabby cursed, swinging around a corner, a corner that he took too wide.

Tabby lay on the ground. It felt like warm beach sand. The sky was too white. Faint sounds surrounded him. People were there but he couldn't see.

"Somebody call an ambulance!" a man shouted; Tabby never heard the yell.

"That is Tabby, boy!" Oh gorm somebody call he wife!"

A dog licked Tabby as it passed his mangled body, and although no one saw, he smiled, feeling the comfort of the warm tongue. Tabby's eyes closed as his last breath escaped his now peaceful body.

The Adjustable Shoe

The Whittakers left their forest home a few years ago, so your parents might be more familiar with their story. Back then the family of five (there was the father: Otto; the mother: Jenny; two sons: Luke and Donnie; and Zorida, a pretty little girl who wore her hair in ponytails) lived in a forest of many moods and smells, some pleasant, others gloomy and unsettling but the loveliest was jasmine at twilight. Their home was a tumbledown house a lot smaller than your bedroom with no windows or gallery. At the front door was a barrel of water fed by a spout for bathing. Surrounding the open yard were trees so large and tall that they never stirred unless the wind howled terribly. The Whittakers' closest neighbour was George Sampson, an old man with no teeth who lived two miles to the south, and he too had neither pipe-borne water nor electricity. The Whittakers, as you would have realised, were terribly poor and should you ever dream about visiting their old home, for the house still stands, prepare for a two-hour walk along a dirt track canopied by thick forest, wear rubber boots and be on the constant lookout for deadly snakes.

After thirty-three years of living in this poverty Mr. Otto Whittaker had had enough so he shaved his head with the razorblade he used on his face and became an inventor. First, he invented a twisted backyard shed built with cedar posts behind the family's home and dubbed *The Inventor Workshop*. Half of the roof remained uncovered. As Otto poked around the yard with dogs and fowls and collected metal, bottles and wood, often working in silence from dusk to dawn, his pregnant wife and three children stood at the front door and marvelled, whispering to each other about *the change*. On the second week of *the change*, long after her fascination had dwindled, Mrs. Jenny Whittaker, his pregnant wife, went to the front door and shouted:

"Otto, where are you? What are you doing?"

"Collecting *Inventor Items*!" His voice came through the mist hanging among the trees.

Shielding her eyes, Jenny squinted and scanned southwest. No sign of Otto. Inside, on the bed, Luke, the eldest child, lay awake between his sleeping siblings, Donnie and Zorida. He was a logical lad, twelve years old, with legs like a bow, a bit lean and short for his age.

"Go tell your father to collect eggs," his mother said, "and don't forget your slippers."

Luke stepped outside, shouting for his father whom he eventually found in *The Inventor Workshop*. Below the shed were an *Inventor Table*, a reed chair and a scrap pile Otto had nicknamed the *Inventor Heap*. Further back were oil drums, a concrete table for cleaning meat, rows of vegetables and a scarecrow fitted with an overturned paint bucket for a head.

Luke sat on the edge of the chair and crossed his feet below it. His father smiled with him, picked up a broken fan blade and began spinning it with his index finger.

"What are you building, Father?"

Otto's eyes grew more intense and his lips pursed. "Do you see those four drums?" He pointed. "I'm building a submarine."

Luke looked at his father sideways. "Where are you going to float it?"

"I don't know," Otto admitted. His look hadn't changed. He was stout despite his poverty, for he worked hard and ate lots of provisions. "What do you think I should build?"

Luke looked at his feet. "Well dad, except for your garden boots none of us have shoes."

Otto closed his eyes and shook his head for he felt ashamed. "I have thought of this already," he cried, "but I do not have enough leather to make shoes for your mother, Zorida and Donnie."

Suddenly, Luke had a brilliant idea which he explained: "Perhaps we should make a shoe that can fit everyone."

Otto loved the idea. He leaped to his feet and began tumbling the *Inventor Heap* with such mad, infectious excitement that Luke joined the search. Otto picked up rubber strips and shouted like a boxing announcer:

"*Inventor Item* number one!"

Otto found twine at the base of the heap and using his jersey as a basket placed it beside the rubber, exclaiming:

"*Inventor Item* number two!"

Jenny shouted something inaudible from the front but Otto didn't respond; grinning at Luke, he made a mischievous face and tapped his forefinger against his lips. Otto arranged the *Inventor Items* he had found in the *Inventor Heap* as if they were for sale: rubber, twine, thread, screws and bolts. He removed a cardboard box from below the table and sifted through its contents, examining each article. The straps of tanned leather were at the bottom. He smelled them one by one, and Luke screeched:

"*Inventor Item* number six!"

The sun came up while Otto scrawled his plans on the *Inventor Table* with a pencil. With breakfast came eggs, porridge and watery tea served in peeling enamel utensils which Jenny brought to *The Inventor Workshop*.

"We need milk, food supplies and candles," she said, staring at her husband.

"Tomorrow," Otto replied without looking at her.

She made an angry face and disappeared inside with the wares when he and Luke had eaten. Otto pulled his stool closer to the table and sat. He clapped his hands, rubbed them together until they became hot and exclaimed:

"Time to invent!"

First, he cut the rubber into two rectangles the length and width of his forearm. Then, using the same scissors he had trimmed his hair with, he carved the rubber pieces into symmetrical pairs and laid them side by side. He leaned over and placed his palms flat on the *Inventor Table*. His eyes grew more intense but he didn't know what he should do next. He was as clueless as a person hearing a foreign language.

"You need a flexible material," Luke said, assisting his father, "so the shoe can lengthen, shorten or widen."

Otto squinted some more, pursed his lips, bobbed his head. After searching the *Inventor Heap* he returned to his stool and sat. He held thin, cylindrical sticks like whips.

"Fibre glass rods," he said anticipating Luke, and laboured on in silence.

Luke knew the material wasn't flexible enough but he didn't comment for his father enjoyed working in silence. After sawing the rods in two, Otto measured them against the pieces of rubber. They were the same length but something was wrong. Scratching his head with both hands he turned to his son and shrugged.

"Fibre glass rods wouldn't work," Luke said, picking up a matchbox. "We need a frame design that can slide back and forth like this matchbox."

Two hours later, Luke and his father were still inventing. Inside the house, ten-year-old Donnie woke with money on his mind. Zorida, age seven, was sitting at his feet reading a bible with no cover. What a bookworm, Donnie thought. He tapped her lightly on her head, laughed and darted outside barefooted; she would have to tidy the bed being the last one off. Donnie said good morning to his mother who had wooden clothespins in her mouth and was hanging clothes on a line that ran from a nail above the front door to a guava tree.

"Go 'n' pu' on y'u' slippers," she mumbled.

"I don't know where they are," he replied. "Is Otto going into the village today?"

Jenny took the pins out of her mouth. "Who are you calling Otto, boy? Yes, he has to go for supplies."

On his way to the garden Donnie acknowledged Otto and Luke. He shook his head at their half-hearted response: they were always pounding some nonsense in the *Inventor Workshop*. Up in the garden he walked carefully between the beds harvesting heads of lettuce and cabbage. Ignoring the midday sun on his back he worked with the idea of stiff, smooth dollar bills; he dreamed of owning a blue hundred dollar, just one. When he had secured the lettuce and cabbage in a box, he removed the scarecrow's tin head, skipped beyond the garden and dug yams from the earth, filling the pan he had with about five pounds worth of produce, a whooping twenty dollars reward. Otto hadn't noticed Donnie but on seeing him returning from the garden laden with vegetables, he scoffed at his shrewdness for now he had no choice but to dismiss inventing.

Luke remained behind in *The Inventor Workshop*.

After walking for one hour Otto and Donnie reached a clearing with fruit trees and a shack that stood on four concrete columns. Two windows flanked the front door and bat droppings smudged the walls. Barrels with rain water all around. The top half of the double door swung open and the Whittakers' closest neighbour stuck his head outside. Mr. George Sampson, a sallow man of eight-five years with sunken features, cloudy eyes and skin like burnt parchment, was Jenny's father. He had white, bohemian hair that looked borrowed and wore a red trucker's cap and rubber boots like Otto's. Wherever he went he took an old dog-eared copybook cluttered with musical notes written for the steelpan in his back pocket. He spoke with abrupt pauses between words and emphasised every one as if angry; perhaps because he was a soldier in his younger days although Otto didn't exactly believe that.

"Who is tha' there? Otto is tha' you? Where's you' hair?"

"George, really, who else could it be?" Otto asked, his sarcasm blatant. He usually spoke to his father-in-law as if he were a child for he felt the old man had to be insane: only crazy folks wrote music for an instrument they had never played nor owned.

George squinted at Donnie. "Which boy is tha' with you? The one who like' money?"

Donnie nudged against his father because George's bulging eyes and egg-sized Adam's apple terrified him. He thought the old man smelled like his shack – like upright crocus bags of eddoes and provisions harvested yesteryear.

"Tell your grandfather good afternoon," Otto said.

Donnie murmured pleasantries but winced when George grinned, flaring his pink gums. George stepped outside with a cooking gas tank, hefted it to his shoulders as easily as if it were a doll and snapped the door shut.

"I am ready," he said.

The group walked in silence except for George who led the way holding the tank with both hands across the back of his neck and humming a *nameless* masterpiece he had been composing for the last fifty years. Donnie trudged behind his father, his eyes trained on Grandfather George and the black pouch tied to his waist, listening to the coins jingling there. With each step the trail widened and brightened but remained tough. George stopped walking and sniffed the air when a brutish animal smell wafted through the forest.

"You all smell that?" he asked. "Tha' is a wild hog!"

"Huh? At last you've stopped humming your crazy music," Otto scoffed for he had walked for two miles thinking only of his inventions.

"You wait and see, you hear?" George snapped, "One day my music will have an audience."

After quarter-of-a-mile they came to a spot where the steepness decreased and the population of bamboo trees crisscrossing over the path increased. Just off the trail two men were dumping a refrigerator on a steep mound of trash Otto visited whenever he needed materials for the *Inventor Heap* in his backyard. There was a third man standing at the base with a shotgun pressed against a pitbull's skull. The men nodded at Otto but didn't return his wave; he allowed Donnie to walk ahead. Another twenty metres or so later the group stepped onto a paved road littered with gravel and stopped to rest but George, anxious to beat sundown, remained standing with the tank against his neck.

"People continue to dump their rubbish in the forest," he complained. "They have no respect for *Papa Bois*."

"You saw the man with the gun?" Otto asked. George nodded; Donnie, marvelling at civilisation in the plains and the primary school under construction, shook his head. Suddenly, there was a gunshot. The boom came in waves that seemingly rustled the vegetation.

"Come, let us go, you hear?" George said.

They continued down the slope, Donnie keeping his distance from his grandfather and thinking of Lakpat, the Chinese shopkeeper with expressive hands who, like him, was a whiz with numbers and fingering money, although the only English words he knew were "bag," "money" and "no-change."

While the group made their way to Lakpat's shop, Luke was sitting in *The Inventor Workshop* inventing. In the forest the hour seemed later and the green land smelled of hog plum and mangoes. Zorida sat on the edge of the reed chair browsing through the coverless bible, her ears alert for papa's voice, for whenever he went out she wasn't allowed in the workshop. She sighed. Without looking up Luke asked:

"Finished reading?"

"For the hundredth time," she replied.

Luke smiled: by some marvel seven-year-old Zorida had taught herself to read. Grandfather George, who knew how to, always denied teaching her. Mother had once caught Zorida hiding beneath a coverlet reading birth certificates. That night everyone learnt their birth date then mother sealed the documents in a plastic bag, found a new hiding spot and warned Zorida never to touch them again.

When she darted off Luke swiped sweat from his neck and face. Where was he again? Using hollow pieces of aluminium he had constructed the frame of the shoe. He smiled to himself as he turned a key that adjusted the shoe's length. An anticlockwise turn on another key widened it. Fully-extended the shoe measured size twelve. Finally, he hefted it and was glad that he had used aluminium instead of steel. Satisfied with his design, he completed the pair. Next, Luke offered up the leather and rubber pieces against the frame. He paused, for although the frame was adjustable the leather and rubber weren't. He hadn't considered that. He closed his eyes, rubbed them and exhaled.

His little sister re-entered *The Inventor Workshop*.

"Zorida, what is a material that could lengthen and shorten at will?"

"Rubber bands, elastic and Velcro. But they're no good. *Real* shoes have leather bodies and rubber soles."

Luke had never heard of Velcro. But he would use a similar concept. Inside the house he managed to sneak rubber bands from the bag with the birth certificates and a little money. In the shed, he verified that the rubber soles were the maximum length and breadth of the frame. Great! *For each frame*, there were six pieces of leather: four pieces for the sides, instep and sole; one for the tip; and one for the heel. Tomorrow, so the shoe could truly be adjustable, he'd cut the rubber and leather pieces in half, bore holes in the ends that met and use rubber bands to reattach them. Then he'd stitch the "adjustable" material to the frame. He hid his work for darkness had fallen.

Inside, Jenny had finished cooking but the twin stove was still burning as the kerosene and candlesticks had exhausted themselves; shadows clawed up the wall and onto the galvanise roof. Now, lying on the mattress she and Otto slept on, one hand on her stomach, the other patting Zorida, she thought mostly of her poverty. Her children, underfed and unschooled, suffered because of her poverty. Jenny closed her eyes, exhaled and prayed. How ironic, she thought, that poor people could have rich faith.

With her eyes still closed Jenny listened to Luke bathing; the hollow sound of the dipper hitting the cold barrel water and her son's grunt as the silver liquid caressed his head and fell to the earth like pebbles on steel. She imagined him shivering and must have chuckled for Zorida stirred beneath her. Luke entered and for a moment the room smelled like soap. Behind the cotton curtain separating the mattresses on the floor, she saw his silhouette dry and dress itself and he would have forgotten to eat and pray had she not reminded him. After, he went right off to bed.

At eight o'clock the nocturnal creatures suddenly stopped crying. Otto entered holding Donnie (agape and sleeping on his shoulder), a small bucket filled with pigtail and red roses with long stems wrapped in damp newspaper; Zorida fretted in bed then turned on her stomach, smacking her lips. Otto grumbled about the unattended fire burning on the stove while Jenny took Donnie and arranged the children in bed, placing Luke in the centre. Otto presented the bare necessities to Jenny then sat on the front step and began removing his boots.

"I couldn't afford the rice," he confessed, securing his boots inside the front door. "But I have good news."

"You will tell me in a moment." Jenny placed both hands on her stomach. "How is my father?"

"Still crazy," Otto replied. Using the strength of his hands he crossed one leg and massaged his instep. "Can you bring me some water?"

On the bureau was a white bucket with rain water. A solitary tin cup floated on top. Jenny scooped and poured a drink into a cream, flaky enamel cup but Otto indicated that she should drink first. When she passed him the water he said:

"Thank you."

After drinking he stood and poured himself another cup. Standing before Jenny he wiped his face and head and smiled. "I got a job, honey."

"Really? Where?"

"From Lakpat! He wants me to work as a shopkeeper."

Jenny's expression hadn't changed. "How come?"

"I don't know. It must be my haircut." Otto ran his hands over his prickly skull and laughed in the darkness. "Lakpat said, 'You wo'k fo' fou' hund'ed dolla', no mo'e no less.'"

Jenny shrieked because, "Four hundred dollars!" had an infinite ring to it.

"Donnie said so also," Otto laughed. "Come, let's lock up and lay in bed." Before he dozed off, he kissed Jenny playfully on her cheeks for the first time in months.

When Luke awoke the next morning Otto had already left for work and Zorida sat at the foot of the bed with Donnie, reading the crumpled newspaper page which had wrapped the roses Otto brought Jenny. Mother was preparing a basket of dirty linen to take to the river, two minutes away, with a smile plastered to her face.

"Good morning Luke," she chirped.

Luke sat up. "Good morning everyone."

Zorida smiled her greetings.

Donnie said, "Pay no attention to him, Zorida. Continue reading."

Jenny had Donnie apologise, and Zorida, worried that she too would be scolded, whispered good morning. Smiling, Luke clapped his hands, rubbed them together until they whistled and exclaimed:

"Time to invent!"

"Not before you eat," Jenny scolded.

That February afternoon, just after lunch, while the island celebrated carnival in the streets, Otto was offloading bags of rice from a truck; Jenny, accompanied by two dogs, was returning from the river with a basin of clothes pressed against her hip; Luke was placing the final, masterful stitch on his invention; and Zorida and Donnie were still sitting on the mattress rereading a newspaper article. Donnie kept muttering, "Ten thousand dollars for a creativity competition? Unbelievable!" But the numbers meant nothing to Zorida so to clear his head he left her and found himself pacing the yard.

In *The Inventor Workshop*, Luke stood inspecting his invention at eye level, clunky pieces like boxes rather than footwear. Should he call his mother and siblings? No! He inhaled deeply and slipped on a pair of shoes for the first time in his life. Way too big and the rubber soles were uncomfortable. Through the padding the aluminium tracks felt uncomfortable, as if standing on pencils. The leather covering wasn't that bad. He bent at the waist and simultaneously turned the keys at the tips; the shoe shortened. Adjustments to the keys on the heels made the shoes narrower. The invention felt most uncomfortable. He waved Donnie into *The Inventor Workshop* and called for Zorida. The results were fascinating. Zorida giggled when Luke slipped her feet inside and adjusted the shoes to a comfortable fit.

"The leather and rubber soles looks like an accordion," Donnie noticed.

Luke sighed. "Yes, that happens when the shoes are small."

"But Luke the pleats look stylish," Zorida said, walking around the *Inventor Table*. "High heels would be nice."

"Girls!" Donnie snapped. "Luke seriously, these shoes can make us rich."

"We still need to test it on an adult," Luke shrugged.

Ignoring Luke, Donnie nodded at Zorida, "Tell him about the creativity competition," and she recited the newspaper excerpt they had been reading earlier as if it were poetry:

"Ministry of Culture, Creativity Competition: pieces are welcome from entrants twelve and over and may include essays, poetry, *inventions*, recorded songs and videos. Entries submitted after February 28th will not be considered. All entries must include a title along with the creativity piece and the sender's return address. Only one entry can be submitted per entrant."

Zorida concluded with the first prize and an address for the Ministry.

"You heard that?" Donnie said, nudging Luke's arm. "First prize is ten thousand dollars!"

Luke whistled.

"Don't you want to submit your shoe?" Donnie asked.

Shocked, Luke stuttered, "This junk isn't even good enough to win second place." But his curiosity mounted. "When is the 28th?"

"Next week," Donnie said. "This *shoe* could win."

"But we don't even have a return address," Zorida said bluntly and Luke and Donnie laughed because that had never occurred to them.

"We will use Lakpat's address," Donnie said.

And so, with permission from their parents and on the condition they had the money to post it themselves, Donnie retrieved his savings of forty-five dollars from the same bag with the birth certificates and other *lawyer stuff*; Otto marvelled; Jenny threw her hands up and said:

"You never know what your kids are up to!"

The following morning Otto pressed Lakpat for permission to use his address but at the post office he learned that forty-five dollars wasn't enough money to mail the package. Dejected, he returned to Lakpat's shop and purposed to spend Donnie's money on food supplies but Lakpat scolded him severely and insisted that he hand-deliver the package. Otto taxied to the capital, a foreign land bustling with noise and impolite faces, and so tree-less and bright he desired to return home. He marvelled when he saw a new hotel with a gold theme and a sign boasting *The International*. Pedestrians on their way to work regarded Otto with disdain, carving around him like a knife when they could but Otto with his country innocence missed the scornful eyes and upturned noses and continued on his way clutching the invention against his chest. At the end of a nameless street he saw a vagrant on his knees sapping his head with water from a canal as if it were a barrel. As fate would have it he met a kind soul (a woman from the country who knew the city extremely well) who took him by car to the Ministry of Culture where he hand-delivered the entry titled:

The Adjustable Shoe.

"How soon will we get a response?" Otto asked the receptionist who collected the entry.

"You will get a letter in July," the receptionist replied, "only if the entry is in the top twenty winners."

Otto's heart sank and didn't surface until May when it seemed that everyone else except Luke had forgotten about the *The Adjustable Shoe.* During this time Otto worked from Sunday to Sunday. Lakpat's store was a combination grocery and rumshop separated by a wooden partition. After lunch on Sundays, Otto spread sawdust on the dirt floor although he thought this quite foolish for the place stank by midweek. In front was an unpaved terrace set with cheap metal chairs and tables, a favourite among the carousers even when the sawdust inside was still fresh.

Donnie went to work with his father every day, sat on the counter with his hands wrapped around his knees and watched him serve patrons. The child spoke only when his father requested totals, for Otto, the man who had planned to build a submarine, couldn't comprehend the abacus Lakpat kept on the counter. On Fridays, after the construction workers had finished toiling on the school they huddled together, noisy, happy and thirsty and demanded rum, beer, "hard wine" and music but Lakpat didn't even own a stereo. Whenever someone cursed Otto stopped whatever he was doing, rocked back his shoulders and snapped:

"What's that? It has a partition true but children and women come here." And Donnie, hidden on the far end of the counter, would giggle when he added, "Look, you made my *little* boy cry."

And the merry drinkers would respond: "Ah Otto, you whine too much! Come buy us a round of drinks."

"Buy all of you drinks?" Otto would exclaim. "No way, partners, I have a family to take care of."

Lakpat on the other hand never bothered with fussy customers. He neither attended to the carousers in the "rumshop section" nor did he stir when they cursed (Donnie wondered if he even knew the bad English words) but he always handled the money, working in silence with his head down and chin stuck to his chest like a servant. When Lakpat worked the abacus, his china eyes narrowed as he slammed beads here and there but once he made a silly error which Donnie recognised.

There was a plump mulatto boy, a bit proud and haughty, whose stepfather sent him daily to the shop with forty dollars to buy a beer, half pack of cigarettes and ginseng. Lakpat sold him without discrimination. The boy always bought mango preserves and fried plantain chips with the change. One day, to Donnie's surprise, this proud mulatto boy purchased a pack of plums along with the regular items, and even though Lakpat used the abacus he returned the usual change. Donnie coughed.

"Chine'e man," the boy argued, sifting through his change, "I think you owe me money."

The shopkeeper's eyes tightened and after fanning out the money like cards on the counter, his singsong English surprised Donnie when he said, "No, you have mo'e money fo' me," and retracted the outstanding amount. Squinting still, he stared at Donnie and grinned slyly.

Lakpat's shop bustled with customers and on Fridays a Syrian merchant came, dripping with sweat and dragging behind him two suitcases stuffed with belts, church shoes and sneakers. He had a loud voice and a commanding accent and he never smoke or drank. Donnie wondered whether he and Lakpat had some business arrangement but the tall, broad-shouldered man always arrived unannounced and heaved his luggage onto the counter with a grunt, and having sensed his arrival the construction workers would surround him and bargain loudly. In the end he and his customers were always happy for unlike his Chinese counterpart he gave credit without regard to race, class or reputation, collecting payments in weekly instalments.

Otto observed these transactions in silence but despite the thin smile on his face, he was sad as he couldn't purchase shoes for his wife and children. He had flatly refused when the Syrian offered him credit; his salary he reasoned was sufficient only for basic household supplies and often while he worked, he pondered how they had survived for so long without a steady income. This made him feel guilty.

Every night after closing the shop, Otto and Donnie left for home. They stopped at Grandfather George's place, Donnie said good evening from a distance and Otto gave the old man that day's newspaper; he always had another under his arm for Zorida.

One Friday in late July when the sun shone fiercely but the sky promised scattered showers and Lakpat's shop smelled of pigtail, a post lady brought him a letter. Donnie was sitting on the counter.

"Fro' China?" Lakpat smiled, opening the letter. "Fo' me?" He sighed and stared at Donnie. "First you' grandfather want' his mail here, now yo'r fat'er too. Next t'ing whole vil'age want mail here." He tossed the letter at Donnie.

Later that night the forest was cold and damp. Luke was standing at the front door rubbing his arms and thinking about the vegetable garden when a beam swiping darkness from between the trees caught his attention. He stared, listened and only relaxed when he heard Donnie's voice. Moments later after saying goodnight and removing his father's boots, he and Donnie, careful not to wake Zorida, lay down. Donnie tossed the opened letter Lakpat had given him at Luke. "*The Adjustable Shoe* came 26th," he whimpered. Luke jerked upright then lay down again and as he cried himself to sleep, Donnie squeezed his eyes shut and wept with him.

Next morning Zorida woke after dawn, knelt and prayed aloud between her sleeping brothers. "Good morning, mother," she said, standing, rubbing her eyes.

"Good morning, Sunshine," her mother replied. "Your father brought you something last night while you were asleep."

"Really?" Zorida shrieked. "What is it?"

On the table, next to the kerosene lamp, were a newspaper and a new bible. Zorida squealed and began perusing the pages, reading aloud but slowly for her mother. Having awakened, Luke and Donnie sat up in bed. Zorida noted their red, puffy eyes and declared:

"Let not your hearts be troubled."

"*The Adjustable Shoe* came 26th," Luke said and disappeared into the garden without breakfast.

"What's wrong with him?" Jenny asked.

Donnie passed the letter to Zorida who read it silently while he made the bed.

"Donnie, can't you read?" she joked and as he pulled the bed sheet tight under the mattress, she continued, "The letter was *posted* on the 26th, dummy – sorry mom, I really meant Donnie. *The Adjustable Shoe* came 2nd in the competition!"

Donnie yelped with delight and rushed into the garden where Luke stood staring at the scarecrow. At first he didn't respond to Donnie's cries but when the news registered and Donnie had convinced him by repeatedly shouting, "Luke, *The Adjustable Shoe* came 2nd!" Luke screamed until his throat ached and the boys hugged each other and did a funny sort of dance that made their mother and sister weak with laughter.

Luke stopped suddenly. "What is second prize?"

Donnie scratched his head and looked at Zorida who shrugged.

The following day Otto telephoned the Ministry from a payphone outside Lakpat's shop. Later, an anxious Jenny, Luke, Donnie and Zorida were waiting at home.

"The second prize," Otto bellowed, "is two nights at the recently opened, magnificent *International Hotel* for up to four persons!"

Above the applause Donnie noted, "But there are five of us."

"You can take the children," Otto said to Jenny, "because I saw the hotel when I went into the city."

"I want daddy to go," Zorida cried.

"Zorida, baby," Otto sighed.

"We can't go without you," Luke said.

"You all will only be gone for the weekend," Otto smiled. "Go. Enjoy it for me."

"No," Jenny said. "We all go or no one goes even if we have to sacrifice the prize."

Within moments their joy had turned to a strange kind of happy sorrow until Zorida said, "Let us pray."

When they lay down to sleep Luke and Donnie whispered excitedly below the blanket until dawn.

To everyone's disappointment Otto could only afford to take his eldest son to the awards ceremony the following evening. Luke wore Lakpat's red changpao (a traditional Chinese garment with a round collar band and horseshoe-shaped sleeves) which extended from his shoulder to heel and a pair of rubber slippers. A friendly customer overjoyed by the historical win lent Otto a shirt, pants and pair of dress shoes. At the entrance a lady fastened orange bands around their wrists. Before Luke left to sit with the prize winners Otto stooped in front him.

"Are you nervous?" he asked, dusting his son's shoulders.

The boy nodded.

"Do you remember the agreement we made as a family?"

"Yes daddy."

"Good. I'm proud of you, son. You look marvellous! Now go!"

Luke went to the front row where nineteen "inventors" sat on padded chairs with red, white and black covers, sweating under bright, yellow lights and tapping their feet anxiously. The stage had the same theme. Overhead, alternating strips of red, white and black silk crisscrossed and drooped at the centre. Light shone through this sun-like pattern. To Luke's great surprise, Grandfather George was sitting in the front row. He smelled like soil and wore a red cap, old tuxedo and bowtie, stiff and brown with dust.

"What are you doing here?" George shouted in his usual abrupt way. "Who brought you here?"

"Shouldn't I be asking you that, grandfather?"

"I came 1ˢᵗ in the competition, you hear?" George said.

"What?" Luke shouted but noticing cold stares he whispered, "What are you going to do with ten thousand dollars?"

"What are you going to do with two nights at a fancy hotel?" George grinned. "Because after tha' it is back to the bush!"

Luke smiled. "How did you win?"

"Wait and see," George responded.

The lighting dimmed but brightened onstage and the awards ceremony opened with great fanfare. The master of ceremonies was a former Ms. Universe. She wore a green dress that sparkled. Behind her a giant television duplicated her movements. With the voice of an angel, she warned the crowd against flash photography. She said a long prayer. A remarkable little girl came onstage, whistled the national anthem without flaw (almost as if playing a flute) and left without a word. Luke remained dazzled at the elegance of the place, the huge stage and the flashing lights. He tried to remember every move and noise of the Chinese acrobats who balanced plates on sticks, the pretty Syrian belly dancer, the energetic African performers, the caucasian lad who juggled up to six knives at a time and the colourful East Indians whose wrists and ankles jangled with each snake-like move; later, Luke would recite everything to his mother and siblings. After a cryptic speech by the Minister of Culture, a judge distributed consolation prizes to the individuals who had placed from fourth to twentieth.

The master of ceremonies came onstage again and summoned Jack Ramoutar, an old man who coughed without pause, to demonstrate his third place invention: *The Snore Box.* When he announced he and his wife always argued because of his midnight and early morning grunting, Luke and the crowd erupted with laughter; he even oinked.

The master of ceremonies brought his invention onstage. It was only an ordinary box with a pipe like a muffler attached but to everyone's surprise it flipped open at the bottom and the man stuck his head inside. After some adjustments he joked, "Listen carefully because I'm about to grunt." Jack Ramoutar shut the box and oinked; and when he did no one heard him, not even the microphone outside. But, true enough, a camera mounted inside the padded contraption showed Jack grunting. After, a technician came onstage and played the recording of the deep, pig-like sounds Jack had made while his head was inside *The Snore Box.* Before Jack returned to his seat, he announced that future versions would include a feature for smokers and flat screen televisions.

The Snore Box amused people but while Luke clapped and laughed heartily he thought the congratulatory applause a bit scanty; George, sitting with his hands on his knees, never budged but continued staring in a most ceremonious manner.

Now when the master of ceremonies announced *The Adjustable Shoe,* Luke froze but the beautiful lady noticed this and encouraged the crowd to repeat his name; as the noise grew louder and the rhythm faster, Luke stood with his grandfather's help, removed his slippers and walked onstage where the lights shone so brightly he couldn't see the people chanting his name. Luke relaxed for now he felt nothing else existed but the master of ceremonies, himself and *The Adjustable Shoe* sitting in a box on the table. The crowd erupted in applause and as the noise died there were murmurs of amusement for if you remember Luke wore a Chinese changpao and had removed his slippers.

In the audience, Otto shouted, "That's my son!"

"You have a handsome son," the master of ceremonies responded heartily. Before tilting the microphone towards Luke she asked, "My dear young inventor, how old are you?"

"Thirteen in September," Luke blushed.

"And where do you live, Luke Whittaker?"

"Deep in the forest," he said innocently, "so deep that we have no address and the postman never comes."

In the crowd pockets of darkness chuckled.

"Never mind them," the master of ceremonies smiled. "What are you going to demonstrate for us today?"

The boy confirmed: "*The Adjustable Shoe.*"

"Is this why you are barefooted?"

Luke nodded.

"The stage is yours, Luke."

When Luke opened the box the smell of leather engulfed the stage. He closed his eyes, picked up *The Adjustable Shoe* and held his invention overhead. The audience clapped lightly. Luke said:

"My family and I live deep in the forest where the grass and stones are sharp but we have no shoes except for a garden boots my father and I share."

No one laughed.

Luke adjusted the horizontal and vertical keys, demonstrating how the shoe could lengthen and widen. "When my sister Zorida begins school in September she can wear this shoe," Luke said gaily, "and when my mother Jenny must go to the river to wash or visit Grandfather George she can turn these keys to make the shoes larger."

Luke slipped on both shoes and stood again. He turned the keys and walked across the stage, concentrating with all his might.

"*The Adjustable Shoe* is neither comfortable nor handsome... like I am," he said at one end of the stage and the atmosphere lightened, "but it works, for if my brother must go to work with my father at Lakpat's shop he can make the shoes smaller than they are now." After some adjustments the shoes were absurdly large for Luke. Now, trudging across the stage, he said, "This is how enormous it will be on my father's feet," and everyone laughed along with the young inventor.

Otto, sitting, weeping, erupted in applause when people stood and clapped. But when the master of ceremonies summoned the first place inventor, George Sampson, onstage he almost fainted. The old man grabbed the microphone and holding it upside-down barked:

"My name is George, you hear?"

A steelpan was brought onstage and a microphone placed beneath it; the master of ceremonies placed George's copybook filled with musical notes on the table and hurried away for the old man who had no teeth and smelled like a garden frightened her. To everyone's surprise George shouted for Luke, his grandson, to join him. Somewhat amused, Otto sat up in his chair but his smirk vanished after George knocked two bamboo sticks together and played his composition, a moving melody that stunned the crowd into mute stupor, for what sweet, "old-time" steelpan music, and oh how tender the sight: the old, white-haired inventor playing beside his grandson who had placed second and still wore *The Adjustable Shoe*. After George's performance the master of ceremonies spent more than three minutes begging the crowd to stop clapping and whistling, while Otto nudged folks in the audience, boasting that George was his father-in-law and Luke his son.

"A family of inventors," the master of ceremonies said then indicated that the third place inventor should come on-stage again. "Let's have another hearty round of applause for Mr. George Sampson, Young Master Luke Whittaker and Mr. Jack Ramoutar."

After the prize-giving, George Sampson, Luke Whittaker and Jack Ramoutar lined up for pictures but George complained, for the whole affair of reporters, cameras, flashing lights and noise was alien.

Still grinning for the cameras, Jack Ramoutar joked, "We should put *The Snore Box* on your grandfather," and Luke lost his composure and giggled into his fist.

"May I speak to you?" Luke asked Jack Ramoutar when the happy crowd except for a few reporters had left.

"Sure, how can I help?"

"My family and I," Luke said, "would like to exchange prizes with you."

"But the third place prize is only a money voucher for a small sum! It is nowhere as spectacular as two nights at *The International* which my wife and two daughters would love to visit," Jack Ramoutar exclaimed. But after a sober discussion with the committee's panel, he and Luke reached an agreement.

Three days after Luke's *third place* photograph appeared in local newspapers, journalists, nongovernmental organisations and non-profits swarmed the Whittakers' forest home. Otto (whom a popular features reporter had tracked to Lakpat's shop) and Grandfather George led them. Everyone wore rubber boots, and one young woman dressed in office attire and particularly wide-eyed with fear, glanced around nonstop. When she queried how they did their laundry, Mrs. Jenny Whittaker took her hand and led her on to the river where she laundered clothes. Luke partnered with a young man, showing him around *The Inventor Workshop*. He even convinced him to dismantle and reassemble his digital recorder. Donnie wanted pictures of his garden produce along with Lakpat's address published in the classifieds. Zorida spent her time dodging a hefty, big-breasted journalist who only caught up after promising tons of reading material.

Among the non-profits were a husband and wife team from *The Peace Work Club*. What a gracious pair Mr. and Mrs. Cozier were as Otto showed them around his humble abode. Mr. Cozier was an architect. When the interviews ended, everyone gathered out front and *The Peace Work Club* presented Mr. Otto Whittaker, Mrs. Jenny Whittaker, Luke, Donnie and Zorida with useful hampers. While shaking hands and smiling for the cameras, Mr. Cozier whispered to Otto that he would get the family a new house. Everyone exchanged handshakes and hugs then Otto and Grandfather George led the visitors away. Jenny, Luke, Donnie and Zorida stood at the front door waving until the forest swallowed the wide-eyed journalist.

The following afternoon the Whittakers trekked south and crammed into George's shack. Three lamps hung on the wall.

In one corner was a spanking new steelpan on a stand. George had stepped outside to dump the last bag of ancient provisions. Meanwhile Zorida sat at a table reading a newspaper to her excited family for the *hundredth time*: "Third place inventor woos nation." There was a picture of Luke standing between George and Jack Ramoutar. Luke bowed and nearly knocked over a kerosene lamp. The feature article contained photographs of Otto sharing a light moment with *The Peace Work Club*, Jenny demonstrating her *washing machine*, Luke sitting in *The Inventor Workshop* reassembling the digital recorder, Donnie in his garden leaning against the scarecrow with the paint bucket head, and Zorida giggling and running from the big-breasted journalist. There was also a picture of Grandfather George in his suit and flashing pink gums.

"Grandfather looks *immaculate*," Zorida said and everyone except Donnie laughed.

"I have a surprise for you all!" Otto exclaimed quite suddenly and his wife and children shuddered with excitement. He arranged everyone in a line. "Close your eyes... now open them!"

In front Jenny, Luke, Donnie and Zorida Whittaker were four pairs of shoes.

"You got them!" Jenny exclaimed, hugging and kissing her husband.

"Yes! The Syrian peddler accepted the money voucher!"

"Now we can go to school!" Zorida and Donnie shrieked.

Luke loved his pair but didn't remove his new adjustable shoe.

"I have another surprise!" Otto announced.

George entered and smiled. He didn't flash blunt, pink gums but false teeth that shone even in the flickering light.

Donnie, who had inched back to the wall, ran up to Grandfather George and hugged his waist.

"Any more surprises?" the children chorused.

George nodded and with childish drama presented portions of Chinese food he had purchased. The family huddled together, Otto led the grace then everyone, including George with his sparkling new teeth, feasted. Then, Grandfather George gave each of his grandchildren one hundred dollars. (Donnie would never spend his crisp, blue hundred dollar bill.) He also gave Otto and Jenny an envelope with a tidy sum of money.

That night the children slept next to Grandfather George with their shoes on. Tomorrow they would have a jolly time at the river. In a bed across the room, Otto pressed his ear against Jenny's stomach and listened. Then he kissed her stomach, glimpsed at Luke, Donnie and Zorida then dozed off thinking he heard steelpan notes wafting through the forest.

www.ingramcontent.com/pod-product-compliance
Lightning Source LLC
Chambersburg PA
CBHW021945120726
47992CB00001B/149